Apress Pocket Guides

W0079190

Apress Pocket Guides present concise summaries of cutting-edge developments and working practices throughout the tech industry. Shorter in length, books in this series aim to deliver quick-to-read guides that are easy to absorb, perfect for the time-poor professional.

This series covers the full spectrum of topics relevant to the modern industry, from security, AI, machine learning, cloud computing, web development, product design, to programming techniques and business topics too.

Typical topics might include:

- A concise guide to a particular topic, method, function or framework

- Professional best practices and industry trends

- A snapshot of a hot or emerging topic

- Industry case studies

- Concise presentations of core concepts suited for students and those interested in entering the tech industry

- Short reference guides outlining 'need-to-know' concepts and practices.

More information about this series at https://link.springer.com/bookseries/17385.

Mastering the Snowflake SQL API with Laravel 10

A Comprehensive Guide to Data Cloud Integrated Development

Ronald Steelman

Apress®

Mastering the Snowflake SQL API with Laravel 10: A Comprehensive Guide to Data Cloud Integrated Development

Ronald Steelman
Justin, TX, USA

ISBN-13 (pbk): 979-8-8688-0381-9   ISBN-13 (electronic): 979-8-8688-0382-6
https://doi.org/10.1007/979-8-8688-0382-6

Managing Director, Apress Media LLC: Welmoed Spahr
Acquisitions Editor: Shaul Elson
Development Editor: Laura Berendson
Coordinating Editor: Gryffin Winkler

Cover designed by eStudioCalamar

Distributed to the book trade worldwide by Apress Media, LLC, 1 New York Plaza, New York, NY 10004, U.S.A. Phone 1-800-SPRINGER, fax (201) 348-4505, e-mail orders-ny@springer-sbm.com, or visit www.springeronline.com. Apress Media, LLC is a California LLC and the sole member (owner) is Springer Science + Business Media Finance Inc (SSBM Finance Inc). SSBM Finance Inc is a **Delaware** corporation.

For information on translations, please e-mail booktranslations@springernature.com; for reprint, paperback, or audio rights, please e-mail bookpermissions@springernature.com.

Apress titles may be purchased in bulk for academic, corporate, or promotional use. eBook versions and licenses are also available for most titles. For more information, reference our Print and eBook Bulk Sales web page at http://www.apress.com/bulk-sales.

Any source code or other supplementary material referenced by the author in this book is available to readers on GitHub (https://github.com/Apress). For more detailed information, please visit https://www.apress.com/gp/services/source-code.

If disposing of this product, please recycle the paper

This book, my first book of what I hope to be many more to come, was truly an enjoyable endeavor with new challenges that were both unexpected and exciting to overcome. I would like to dedicate this book to my loving mother, Sheree Burkhart, for always believing in me and always driving me to be my best self; my amazing partner, Rudy Gomez, for his support and encouragement; my niece and nephew, Zeke and Hanna, for giving me some good laughs on the phone when I needed a break; and to the rest of my family for the "home team support" they have shown me.

I'd also like to thank my publishing team at Apress for their hard work and dedication to helping make this book what it is. Without their support and guidance, I'd be just another nameless keyboard warrior.

Finally, I'd like to thank all of you, my readers, who took a chance at this publication. I hope it gives you the knowledge you need to succeed.

Table of Contents

TABLE OF CONTENTS

About the Author

 **Ronny Steelman**, a dynamic author in the field of data, analytics, and programming, brings over 15 years of invaluable expertise to his work. Residing in Dallas, Texas, Ronny's passion for data-driven insights ignited during his time at the University of Oklahoma, where he honed his analytical skills and set the foundation for his illustrious career.

With a visionary spirit and a knack for leading data teams, Ronny has spearheaded transformative projects across various industries. His journey through the ever-evolving landscape of data technology, including starting his own data consulting company, QuadraByte, has not only established him as a thought leader but also fueled his commitment to sharing knowledge. *Mastering the Snowflake SQL API with Laravel 10* is a testament to Ronny's dedication to empowering others with the skills and wisdom gained from his remarkable journey in the world of data. At the age of 35, Ronny's story exemplifies how passion and expertise can converge to shape the future of data analytics.

About the Technical Reviewer

 **Dmitry Anoshin** is a data engineering leader with 15 years of experience working in business intelligence, data warehouse and data integration, big data, cloud, and ML space across North America and Europe. He is currently focusing on raising the bar of data engineering and analytics skills globally with Surfalytics.com.

He leads data engineering initiatives, working on a petabyte-size data platform built using cloud and big data technologies for supporting machine learning experiments, data science models, business intelligence reporting, and data exchange with internal and external partners. He handles privacy compliance and security-critical datasets.

Apart from work, Dmitry teaches a cloud computing course at the University of Victoria, mentors high-school students at the CS faculty, and volunteers his time to coaching people with analytics engineering skills in the CIS region. Moreover, he is an author of analytics books and a speaker at data-related conferences and user groups.

CHAPTER 1

Snowflake

Why Snowflake?

The three founders of Snowflake started the company in July 2012 in San Mateo, California. Within a few years, the company became the leader in cloud data, or "data-as-a-service," as its customer base and investment capital continued to grow at an exponential rate. By 2023, the company's revenue was 2.067 billion US dollars. Although many reasons exist for choosing Snowflake over other cloud data providers, the company leans into its value proposition of increasing customer ROI by 612%, its ability to run over 2.6 billion queries per day, and a rich partner ecosystem of over 1,300 partners. Add to this the platform's growing database driver solution, robust API, unparalleled infrastructure for computing and data, and a growing roadmap of new features, including native support for AI and ML, and it is easy to see the attraction to the platform.

Companies that adopt Snowflake do so because they do not want to take on the overhead and management of database infrastructure and networking uptime, instead choosing to rely heavily on Snowflake's rapid data access, on-demand warehouse initialization, and its tried-and-tested backend infrastructure. Leveraging Snowflake allows companies to do away with most of the DBA overhead required in traditional database solutions by utilizing Snowflake's data warehousing as a service and instead allows companies to focus time, resources, and money on data warehousing, data analysis, and AI and ML initiatives.

© Ronald Steelman 2024

R. Steelman, *Mastering the Snowflake SQL API with Laravel 10*, Apress Pocket Guides, https://doi.org/10.1007/979-8-8688-0382-6_1

As Snowflake has continued to grow, they have adopted the mantra of "one platform with near-unlimited potential." This includes the ability to execute workloads under optimal performance; fully automate the security, governance, and availability; and collaborate securely on a global scale using their data marketplace. Snowflake's unique architectural designs allow businesses to connect globally across clouds in order to mobilize their data and to break down data silos.

What Is the Snowflake API?

The Snowflake SQL API is a RESTful API that anyone can use to access and update data in a Snowflake instance. The API supports the ability to perform query operations, provision users and roles, create tables, and manage many other aspects of your Snowflake deployment. By leveraging API development best practices, Snowflake has enabled users with the capabilities of submitting SQL statements for execution, including most DDL and DML statements, checking the status of any statement execution, canceling a statement execution on-demand, and providing the ability to fetch query results concurrently.

API stands for Application Programming Interface, which is a software intermediary provided by an application to other applications and allows two applications to talk to each other. The RESTful standard stands for REpresentational State Transfer, which is an architectural style. REST defines a set of principles and standard protocols through which APIs can be built around. REST is the widely accepted architectural style of building APIs.

Snowflake employs data partition architecture in its SQL API to help users fetch query results while, under the hood, determining the number of partitions returned and the size of each partition. For added security, the SQL API can be protected by leveraging Snowflake network policies that restrict access to the account where the API is enabled. While being near limitless in its capabilities, some functionality limitations exist, including the ability to use the GET and PUT commands against a Snowflake Stage. Additionally, the SQL API does not currently support stored procedures that leverage the Python programming language.

Snowpark API

In addition to the Snowflake SQL API, Snowflake also provides an intuitive API for interacting with the Snowpark library. Using this API, you can write Snowpark Python code in a local development environment and execute it natively within Snowflake. This allows users to create and leverage Python-stored procedures, leverage powerful Python libraries (such as DataFrame and Pandas), create UDFs and UDTFs, and perform machine learning tasks.

The scope of this book primarily focuses on the Snowflake SQL API, but some chapters will touch upon aspects of the Snowpark API so that users may have a better understanding of the Snowflake API functionality.

For more information regarding the Snowpark API, you can refer to the official Snowpark Library for Python API reference documentation: `https://docs.snowflake.com/developer-guide/snowpark/reference/python/latest/index`.

Why Laravel?

Laravel is a robust PHP framework that provides developers with a lightweight codebase, an extensive package and community ecosystem, and the flexibility to develop at varying levels of model-view-controller (MVC) adherence. When I first started working with the Snowflake SQL API, it was to build our Black Diamond 360 (`https://blackdiamond360.com/`) solution for managing and monitoring a Snowflake instance. Because the platform was built as a multi-tenancy solution, and due to the

3

limited availability of PHP drivers or an out-of-the-box Laravel Snowflake package, our team opted to instead leverage the Snowflake API. This allowed us to more easily design and develop a multi-tenant solution and provided us the additional benefits of the security Snowflake includes with the SQL API.

Most of this book is aimed at providing developers with the knowledge they need to work with the Snowflake SQL API. Because the SQL API is a RESTful API, any programming language or framework can be used that supports REST API calls.

Snowflake SQL API vs. Drivers

If you have any advanced level of exposure to Snowflake, or most database solutions for that matter, you may already be aware of the existence of database drivers. Drivers are a great way to natively support Snowflake within your application. While they have fewer limitations than the SQL API, they do have some shortcomings. First, as of the writing of this book, Snowflake only supports seven drivers (GO, JDBC, .NET, Node.JS, ODBC, PHP PDO, and Python). Second, driver upgrades can mean more intensive testing and code changes that must be made to your application before depreciated versions are enforced.

While drivers play a definite role in many applications, there may be times where you choose to go the route of an API. For example, in our Black Diamond tool, we run a multi-tenant application that allows the customer to connect one or more Snowflake instances to the tool. While doing dynamic configuration loading of a Snowflake connection to the supported driver in Laravel, or other languages, is possible, it does introduce some complexities and even potential security risks.

Other use cases where you might use an API instead of a driver are a little more straightforward. Building native mobile applications for iOS or Android, where the primary application is a web app and the mobile application is a supporting interface, the API can allow you to quickly and efficiently connect to your Snowflake data to pull, push, update, and even delete data. If you are working with integration tools that do not have driver support, or you are working in an environment where installing drivers is a limitation, the SQL API can also help overcome this and allow you access to your data in Snowflake.

In general, in any instance where using a driver might create complications or limitations, the SQL API really starts to shine. But perhaps one of the things I personally like about the API is that Snowflake maintains a Snowflake API status page that can be programmatically queried. In this way, my application can quickly determine if there is an outage at Snowflake and then handle the outage appropriately.

Understanding the Snowflake SQL API Architecture

The Snowflake SQL API was created to provide developers with a lighter-weight option that doesn't require them to install heavy packages, libraries, or drivers or to use languages not supported with existing Snowflake drivers. The API provides a set of endpoints that allow you to issue SQL commands and fetch the results of those commands over Transport Level Security (TLS) protocols standard with HTTP. All results are returned in JSON V2, providing developers with a simple method to build a client from standard libraries available in almost all modern programming languages.

While Snowflake has identified its API as a RESTful API, it does not fit perfectly into the standards defined for a traditional REST API. REST APIs, by definition, have resource endpoints in the form of URLs, which are typically acted upon with HTTP commands (GET, DELETE, PATCH, PUT, etc.). Instead, the Snowflake SQL API only provides a few endpoint URLs that are meant to act as a medium to send SQL statements to Snowflake and retrieve the results over HTTP, similar to an RPC service.

When a user submits a request to the endpoint, the API first determines if it is a valid request. If not, an HTTP error code is returned, and the processing stops. If the request is valid, it creates an HTTP call to the Snowflake instance and submits the query to the processor. The processor then begins to execute the statement and resides in three states. The first state is a "sleeping state" in which the API waits for a set period of time and then checks once again for results. The second state is an error state, in which the statement returns a Snowflake error and is passed back to the API response body as an HTTP error. The final state is a success state in which the API response body returns an HTTP success response and a JSON body of the payload.

In the third state, the successful state, the API response body might also include the reference to additional partitions. Because some datasets may be too large to transmit all at once, Snowflake breaks them up into partitions. Subsequent requests can be made to the Snowflake SQL API to fetch additional partitions, or pages, of data and works similar to how pagination works in most modern programming languages.

To execute a new statement, the developer must construct the body of the HTTP request to pass to the endpoint, including the SQL statement to be executed, and send it to the API as a POST request. Snowflake provides the option to include a custom UUID instead of an auto-generated one to help identify duplicate requests and make partition fetching easier. We will discuss more about how that works later on. You can also indicate if you want to execute the statement asynchronously, allowing custom applications to be more flexible in specifying how query responses are handled.

CHAPTER 2

The Snowflake Data Cloud

Foundations

Before we get into the details of how to use the Snowflake SQL API, it is important to establish some foundational principles for its use. In this book, we sometimes use Snowflake SQL API, Snowflake API, SQL API, and API interchangeably. Unless it is otherwise specified as belonging to another API service, such as the Snowpark API, all three uses refer specifically to the Snowflake SQL API. As Snowflake continues to grow, they have continued to iterate and evolve the Snowflake SQL API and introduce new API libraries for users to leverage, allowing developers to tap into the robust power of Snowflake more easily. As such, the techniques shared in this book may not apply to all products that fall under the Snowflake umbrella.

Understanding Snowflake's Evolution

In addition to the Snowflake SQL API, Snowflake also supports the use of their Snowflake Native App Framework and the Snowpark API. Understanding how these solutions differ from the SQL API will allow

© Ronald Steelman 2024
R. Steelman, *Mastering the Snowflake SQL API with Laravel 10*, Apress Pocket Guides,
https://doi.org/10.1007/979-8-8688-0382-6_2

you to better understand the capabilities that Snowflake provides. In the advanced chapters of this book, we will briefly touch upon both platform capabilities. In order to provide a verbose primer, we will discuss how the two differ here.

Snowpark API

The Snowpark library provides developers with an intuitive library for querying and processing data at scale in Snowflake. The library supports one of three popular AI and machine learning programming options, giving developers the freedom to work in a language they are comfortable with: Python, Scala, and Java. The Snowpark API might be considered an iteration of the Snowflake Connector for Spark, which allows developers to bring Snowflake into the Apache Spark ecosystem. This enables them to use Spark to read data from and write data to Snowflake.

From there, the comparisons start to diverge. Snowpark developers are optionally able to take benefit of interacting with data directly in Snowflake using libraries and patterns purpose-built for different languages while maintaining performance and functionality, support most code IDEs (such as Jupyter, VS Code, and IntelliJ), support for offloading data transformation and heavy lifting (such as Snowflake UDFs) to the Snowflake data cloud, and do not require you to maintain separate work clusters outside of the Snowflake for running computations.

Because of its ability to support these languages natively, developers can use type checking within the native language construct to execute SQL statements or, optionally, choose to specify the SQL statement they wish to execute. A great example of this is the ability to use code constructs provided by the popular Python library, DataFrames, to construct SQL select queries.

Since Snowpark runs natively within Snowflake, all operations are lazy-executed on the server, allowing developers to use the library to delay running transformations until much later in the pipeline while also providing the flexibility to batch multiple operations into a single call. This allows developers to shave down the amount of time it takes to transfer data between your client and the Snowflake database and offers additional performance improvements.

Using the toolbox provided by the Snowpark API, developers can create user-defined functions (UDFs) directly within the Snowpark app. Snowpark can push your code to the server and execute your UDFs at scale on your data. This provides many useful and powerful options for working with data, including looping or batching functionality, where creating a UDF allows Snowflake to parallelize and apply the code at scale within Snowflake.

By defining custom UDFs within your code, you can write functions in the same language that you use to write client code, allowing you to process data directly within the Snowflake database. Snowpark magically handles pushing the custom code for UDFs to the Snowflake database and can be called within your client code. This means you do not need first to transfer data to your local client in order to execute the function on the data, saving you time, code, money, and performance.

Snowflake Native App Framework

The Snowflake Native App Framework allows developers to expand the capabilities of other Snowflake features by sharing data and related business logic with other Snowflake accounts, allows for the sharing of an application with consumers through the Snowflake marketplace as either a free or paid app, and includes feature-rich visualizations using Streamlit. Snowflake does this by allowing you to create data applications that directly leverage core Snowflake functionality.

Snowflake has built its Native App Framework to perform along most development standards, including an easy way to leverage testing environments within your account, a robust developer workflow to manage code within source control while maintaining data and related database objects within Snowflake, the ability to version and patch your applications as they continue to evolve, incrementally release updates to consumers, and support for logging and unstructured events that allows your developers to troubleshoot and monitor applications.

Currently, the Native App Framework has a few limitations that developers should keep in mind. These include limited support (no support on Microsoft Azure or Google Cloud Platform), cross-cloud auto-fulfillment except within certain AWS regions, no support for government cloud–enabled regions, limited single organization support for Virtual Private Snowflake (VPS), requiring users to use sequences instead of AUTOINCREMENT on newly created tables, not supporting temporary tables or stages, limited support of Streamlit, and limitations on references. Snowflake has structured its Native App Framework around a provider-consumer model, which is also used in features such as Snowflake Collaboration and Secure Data Sharing.

To support Native Apps, providers, or a user who wants to share data content and application logic with other users, must follow a specific architecture to enable the code for the application package, assign and maintain licensing and entitlements, provide access to proprietary data, and provide access to App events. Once the application is ready to publish, providers can push the application to the Snowflake Marketplace as a public listing or privately list their application for more controlled access.

A consumer, or a Snowflake user who wants to access the data content and application logic shared by providers, can then go to the listing and enable the application. The application is installed in the consumers' Snowflake instance, is able to be connected to their local data, and can be integrated with a consumer's external systems.

Key Concepts: Data Warehousing in the Cloud

Snowflake Architecture

Snowflake, a self-managed data platform service, enables data storage, processing, and analytic solutions that are faster, easier to use, and more flexible than traditional database offerings. It uses a new, state-of-the-art SQL query engine deployed on an innovative architecture that has been natively designed for the cloud. Because it is a cloud-based service, there is no hardware to choose from or configure and manage and no software to maintain, and ongoing maintenance and tuning are handled directly by Snowflake.

In this section, we will delve into the architectural foundations of Snowflake, one of the most innovative and powerful cloud data warehousing platforms available today. Understanding the architecture is essential for anyone seeking to harness the full potential of Snowflake's capabilities.

A Multitiered, Multi-clustered Approach

At the heart of Snowflake's architecture is its multitiered, multi-clustered design. This unique structure allows Snowflake to seamlessly handle data storage and query processing at scale. The Snowflake architecture primarily includes the storage tier, compute tier, and service tier.

The storage tier is responsible for managing and storing data efficiently in a highly compressed, columnar format. Snowflake's patented object storage, where your data is security stored, can reside in cloud storage services such as Amazon Web Services (AWS), Microsoft Azure, and Google Cloud Platform (GCP).

The compute tier consists of clusters of virtual machines (commonly referred to as virtual warehouses in Snowflake) that handle query processing. Snowflake dynamically allocates and scales these clusters to ensure optimal query performance, even in the face of varying workloads. The compute tier is a consumption-based model consisting of credits, which are consumed based on the amount of time it takes the query to run and the size of the virtual warehouse.

Finally, the service tier acts as the control plane for Snowflake, managing authentication, query routing, metadata storage, and more. The service tier coordinates activities between the storage and compute tiers, ensuring data consistency and integrity.

The Snowflake SQL API allows you to take full advantage of these powerful tiers directly within your application, allowing you the customization and flexibility to build an application the way you want while still gaining the benefits of the Snowflake architecture.

How does Snowflake achieve such an approach? Through the use of a hybrid combination of traditional shared-disk and shared-nothing database architectures. For persisted data that is accessible from the compute tier, Snowflake uses a central data repository. In addition, each compute cluster in the compute tier stores a portion of the entire dataset locally which can then process queries using massively parallel processing. This allows Snowflake users a more simple and familiar form of data management but provides more optimal performance in scale-out architecture.

To handle all of this, Snowflake has three layers unique to their architecture: database storage, query processing, and cloud services. As data gets loaded into Snowflake, the database storage layer converts the data into a compressed columnar format which is then stored in cloud storage. These data objects are not directly visible or accessible by customers and can only be accessed using SQL queries. This includes how the data is organized, the file size of each page of data, the structure, metadata, and statistics. The query execution layer is where all of the data can be accessed by the user, and is run on virtual warehouses using massively parallel processing compute clustering. Virtual warehouses are not shared resources with other Snowflake customers or other virtual warehouses, therefore minimizing any performance impact on processing. In the cloud services layer, orchestration of Snowflake takes place. All of the services offered by Snowflake that are used to process requests on behalf of a user occur in the cloud services layer. This includes authentication, management of Snowflake infrastructure, metadata management, query processing, and access controls.

Snowflake SQL API: A Comprehensive Overview

The Snowflake SQL API, at version 6.3 as of the time of this writing, consists of a single resource and three endpoints. The first endpoint, and also the resource itself, is used to submit SQL statements for execution: */api/v2/statements/*. The second endpoint supported by the REST API checks the status of the statement by passing a unique identifier to */api/ v2/statements/<uuid>*. Finally, statements can be canceled if they are hung, in an infinite loop, or taking too long to pass the unique identifier to */api/v2/statements/<uuid>/cancel*. The SQL API has been designed to remove concurrency limits, which enables you to retrieve query results from multiple threads.

When executing a new SQL statement, a JSON body is created, including the SQL statement, and sent to the endpoint using the HTTP POST method. You can optionally include a UUID in the request; otherwise, Snowflake will automatically generate one on your behalf. It is suggested to use a UUID generator to create your own UUID values in order to make it easier for subsequent API calls, including retries for failed queries. Snowflake allows you to specify if you want to asynchronously execute the statement, both in the request or as a setting within Snowflake.

All requests sent to the API will return a 202 status code indicating that Snowflake has received the request and is processing it. The payload will also include a statement handle and a statement status URL, which can be polled by your code for results. This makes it easy for you to structure your application in such a way as to lazy load your interface and poll the results to be loaded later using functionality such as AJAX or some other JavaScript method.

Polling the results uses the GET HTTP method, and it is recommended to provide a brief delay between requests for results to allow Snowflake the time it needs to fully execute the query and load the results into a response body. Once the results are complete, Snowflake will return a 200 status code along with the first page of the data from the query, as well as additional information you need to pull additional pages (partitions). Because of the flexibility of the API, you have the option to pull additional pages sequentially or in parallel.

CHAPTER 3

Getting Started with Snowflake SQL API

Introduction

This chapter aims to familiarize you with the foundational concepts and essential steps required to effectively utilize the SQL API for your data management and analytics needs. Whether you are a seasoned SQL developer or new to the world of cloud data platforms, this chapter provides the necessary context and hands-on instructions to help you get up and running with Snowflake.

We will begin by exploring the basics of Snowflake's SQL API, including how to connect to the platform and execute your first queries. You will learn how to navigate the Snowflake environment, interact with various database objects, and understand the key components that make up the Snowflake architecture. Additionally, this chapter will guide you through setting up your Snowflake account, configuring your workspace, and importing data, ensuring you have a solid foundation to build upon. By the end of this chapter, you will be equipped with the knowledge and skills to start leveraging Snowflake's SQL API for efficient and effective data analysis.

© Ronald Steelman 2024
R. Steelman, *Mastering the Snowflake SQL API with Laravel 10*, Apress Pocket Guides,
https://doi.org/10.1007/979-8-8688-0382-6_3

Setting Up Your Snowflake Account

Snowflake uses a browser-based web interface for interacting with the platform, as well as a command-line interface (SnowSQL), various database drivers, and API access. If it is your first time getting started with Snowflake, you'll want to log in using the Snowflake web-based client called Snowsight to get started. After registering for an account and agreeing to the Terms of Service, you'll be provided with an email with instructions on logging in for the first time.

Logging into Snowflake uses a unique URL that contains an account identifier. The account identifier is a way to identify your Snowflake account within your organization uniquely and also separates it from the global network of other Snowflake accounts. The account identifier uses your account name along with the organization name (e.g., *myorg-account123*) to reference your unique account. You can optionally use the Snowflake-assigned account locator as the identifier, but this legacy format is discouraged as Snowflake plans to phase it out. You use your Snowflake unique account identifier in a variety of ways, including

1. Accessing the Snowflake web interface via a web browser

2. Using SnowSQL and other clients to connect to Snowflake

3. Third-party applications and services within the Snowflake ecosystem

4. Security features that protect your Snowflake account

5. Global features, such as secure data sharing and replication

6. Accessing the Snowflake SQL and Snowpark APIs

It is important to note that upon initial registration, you'll be given both an account identifier and an organization identifier. Organizations enable administrators within your business to manage all aspects of your Snowflake contract as it relates to your business entity. An organization can have one or multiple accounts attached to it, each with its own unique identifier, giving you the flexibility to set up your cloud data center in a way that meets your business's unique needs. If your business did not sign up through the self-service option, Snowflake will have already created an organization for you and assigned it to your ORGADMIN (the owner of your organization). Account identifiers, including legacy identifiers and other lesser-used formats, are fully detailed in the Snowflake documentation but are outside the scope of this book. We will use the preferred format that Snowflake recommends, but you can see all other formats and information regarding them here: `https://docs.snowflake.com/en/user-guide/admin-account-identifier`

Configuring and Managing Your Environment

To get started, you need to log into your Snowflake environment. You can go directly to the unique URL that was provided by Snowflake when you registered or go to *https://app.snowflake.com* and log in with your account name and Snowflake credentials. Once you are logged into Snowsight, you'll want to navigate to the Admin section in the left-hand navigation bar. From here, we will create a new user for your API. Because of the power of the API, it is not recommended to use a user that has ACCOUNTADMIN or ORGADMIN access.

We will not define a Default Role or a Default Warehouse for now. Go ahead and click Create User and then test that you are able to log in with that user. Once you are finished, log back into Snowsight using your ACCOUNTADMIN credentials, and we will move on to creating your first role. Roles provide you with a simple method to group users into a single team, department, or set of permissions. When you are managing security in Snowflake, you'll *GRANT* access to Snowflake objects directly to a role. Roles work using inheritance, allowing you to create a tree structure for your role to inherent permissions and reduce redundant *GRANTS*. We will create a basic role and assign it to the User we created previously. Ensure the role does not inherit any permissions from other roles unless you need it to. In most cases, it is recommended that your API role does not inherit any permissions from other roles and that the permissions are custom-tailored to what you need your application to perform. This prevents you from opening up too much access and mistakenly removing access that could break your application.

Next, we want to navigate to Warehouses and create a new Warehouse. Based on the structure of your application and business logic, you might have multiple Warehouses that get called in various areas of your application based on resource needs. In large part, however, you should have one Warehouse dedicated to your API user, which is the Default Warehouse. This allows you to incrementally scale and increase the size of your Warehouse as your application grows while not impacting other Snowflake queries. Once you create the new Warehouse, go back to the User we created previously, click Edit, and assign the Default Role and Default Warehouse we just created.

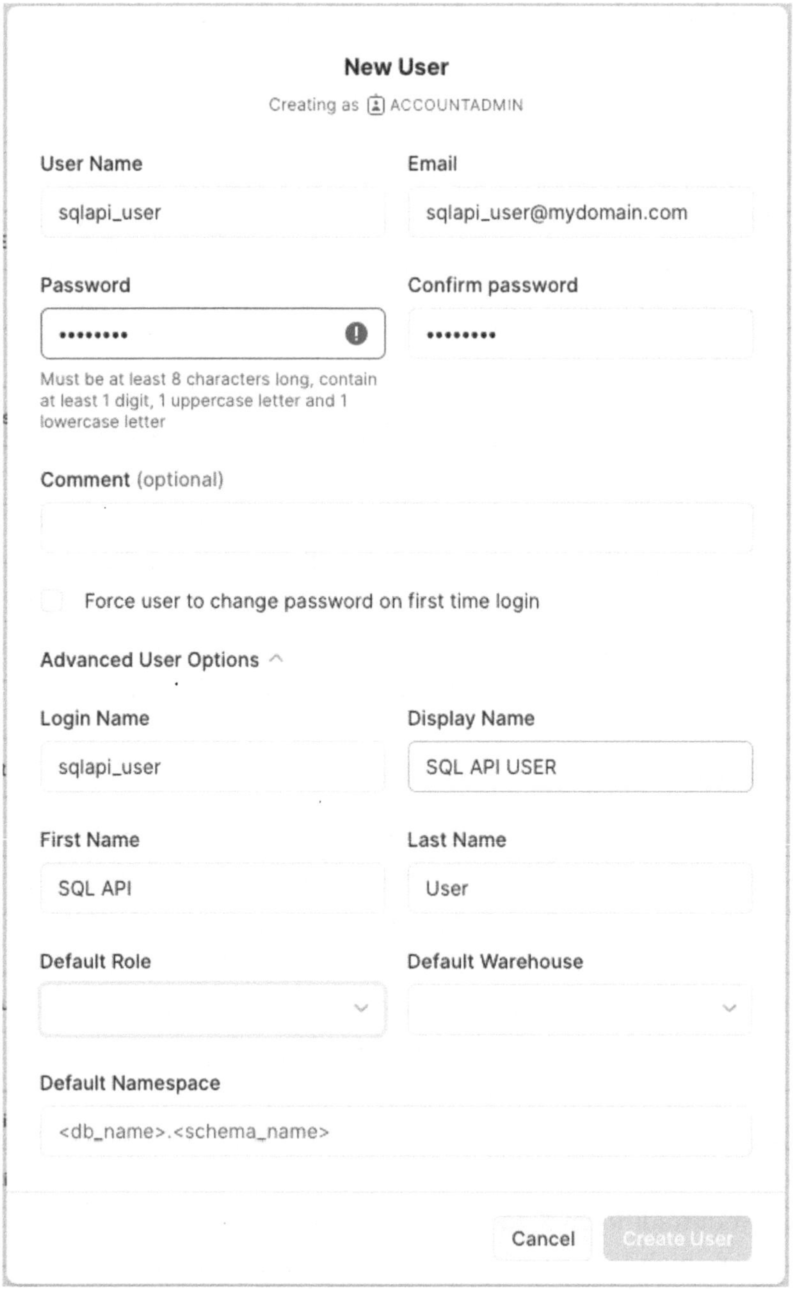

New User

Creating as 🔒 ACCOUNTADMIN

User Name

sqlapi_user

Email

sqlapi_user@mydomain.com

Password

•••••••• ⚠

Confirm password

••••••••

Must be at least 8 characters long, contain
at least 1 digit, 1 uppercase letter and 1
lowercase letter

Comment (optional)

☐ Force user to change password on first time login

Advanced User Options ⌃

Login Name

sqlapi_user

Display Name

SQL API USER

First Name

SQL API

Last Name

User

Default Role

Default Warehouse

Default Namespace

<db_name>.<schema_name>

Cancel   Create User

Figure 3-1. *New user creation*

Navigating the Snowflake Web Interface

Snowflake provides users two primary ways to interact with the Snowflake cloud platform: the SnowSQL command-line utility and the web-based Snowflake UI, referred to as Snowsight. Of the two, the Snowflake Web UI is the most commonly used method for interacting with Snowflake, including executing queries and performing administrative functions such as managing warehouses, database objects, security, and reviewing cost and performance.

Snowflake provides both the Snowsight UI and the Classic UI, but we will focus on the former, considering that the Classic UI has a roadmap to be fully phased out. You are presented with the Dashboards page and a left-hand navigation when logging in. We will discuss each section within that navigation, including submenu items and how they are used when working with Snowflake. This information, though foundational, is essential to understand so that we can better demonstrate the capabilities and communicate the limitations of the Snowflake SQL API.

Dashboard

Dashboards provide Snowflake users with a flexible way to create collections of charges, arranged as tiles, that get populated directly by query results from your Snowflake data. This allows you to build rapid solutions to monitor your Snowflake account as well as derive quick insights into your data that can be used repeatedly and shared with other team members. The dashboard metrics are fully customizable and support a wide range of filtering options to provide interactive, dynamic filtering to the end users. While it is a powerful addition to your arsenal, it should be noted that the Dashboards functionality in Snowflake is not intended to replace your traditional BI tools. Instead, it should be used as a way to gain some quick, high-level insights into your account and data.

Worksheets

Snowflake's Snowsight UI supports a web-based querying tool called Worksheets that behaves similarly to SQL tools such as DBeaver, PHPMyAdmin, pgAdmin, and others. When you first open Worksheets, you'll see a list of your recently opened files and a file explorer on the left-hand of the screen. The file explorer supports the creation and organization of both files and folders, giving you a cloud-based editor. Clicking any file will open it in a new tab, which can be managed along the top of the screen, as well as allowing you to navigate to other open tabs. Using Worksheets, a user can create both SQL and Python Worksheets.

When using SQL Worksheets, you can write and run SQL statements the same as you might using a desktop tool, explore the query results, apply filters, and generate quick visualizations of the query results. For any Worksheet you create, you can modify some standard metadata, such as the title of the Worksheet, and share settings with other users within your Snowflake instance.

Similar to SQL Worksheets, Python Worksheets allows you to execute raw Python code directly within the Snowflake environment. This is a great tool to use that does not require a lot of overhead configuration, like Juypter notebooks, and allows you to run Python directly against your data without first having to download the data and upload the results. Python Worksheets provide you with direct integration to Snowflakes Snowpark tool, unlocking the full potential of Python and, by extension, numerous packages to support artificial intelligence and machine learning programming.

Data

This section covers the Data tab in the navigation pane, which consists of various functional areas specific to the data in your Snowflake instance. Aside from Worksheets, users will spend a large part of their time in this section of Snowsight, performing various data tasks such as database management, data sharing, and governance.

Databases

The Databases section allows a user to take full advantage of the GRANTS given to their current role. Snowflake allows you to change your role on the fly using the option in the top-left corner of the screen and updates the Databases page according to the GRANTS that role has. This is a great way to test what various roles have access to before assigning a user to a role.

The Databases section has a nested navigation panel that allows you to sort through a hierarchical view of databases granted to your current role. This includes the ability to drill down to the lowest level of the database that your role supports. To provide the most verbose explanation of this section, we will assume you are using the ACCOUNTADMIN role, giving you full access to all database objects in your Snowflake instance. Apart from any database you have created in your organization, you'll most likely see two other databases: SNOWFLAKE and SNOWFLAKE_SAMPLE_DATA. The SNOWFLAKE database provides various views and functions that allow you to retrieve a plethora of metadata about your Snowflake instance, including query history, access history, warehouse usage, credit consumption, and more. The SNOWFLAKE_SAMPLE_DATA database provides you with a full dataset of test data that you can use to learn more about Snowflake. Both of these databases are standard to Snowflake and are outside the scope of this publication.

At the top level, clicking on a database name will expand the node for that database and update the information screen with additional details. Database Details outlines any roles that have access to the database along with their explicit privileges, while Schemas will give you a list of the current schemas that belong to the database. In the top-right of the page, you have some additional options that include dropping the database, cloning the database, modifying the database, and transferring database ownership. From this screen, you may also create a new Schema using the "+ Schema" button.

Clicking on any schema in the tree will take you to a Schema Details page listing the roles and privileges granted to the schema. If you are not familiar with how roles work in Snowflake, it is recommended you review the documentation. In short, roles are most restrictive first. If you are granted access to a schema but not the parent database, as an example, you will be unable to view the schema.

Within a schema, you can also see the tables, stages, file formats, and procedures that your role has access to. In the top-right, you have a few options to modify your schema and a "Create" button that allows you to quickly create tables, views, stages, storage integrations, file formats, sequences, pipes, streams, tasks, functions, procedures, and dynamic table using a graphical form editor.

As you continue to go further down the tree into objects such as tables, views, and procedures, you'll find similar object information and editing options. One important thing to note as you drill further into objects is the information screen will now start to show you a definition window, which has the complete SQL query needed to create that object. This is great for debugging your objects or if you need to re-create an object in a new database.

Private Sharing

Private Sharing is a feature that lets you share select data within your Snowflake instance with other Snowflake accounts and potentially monetize your data. Direct Shares under Shared With You will show you any data that is shared to your Snowflake account. Shared By Account will show any data you are currently sharing with other Snowflake customers by specifying direct consumers, publishing to the Marketplace, or creating a Direct Share. The final tab, Reader Accounts, lets you specify data shared to an individual who is not currently a Snowflake customer, giving them read-only access to your data without needing a Snowflake account.

Provider Studio

Provider Studio is a more advanced topic that is beyond the scope of this publication. This allows you to create Snowflake applications and publish them to the Snowflake Marketplace, manage your listings, and view analytics about any application you've listed on the Marketplace. The Learn tab has a number of articles that are great to read if you plan to leverage the Marketplace for publishing applications. Snowflake even provides various ways to collect payment for the use of your published applications, including the ability to use Snowflake credits as digital currency.

Governance

As of this writing, Governance is a relatively new feature in Snowsight. The Dashboard page lets you quickly see how many Snowflake objects you have, any tags and policies assigned to those objects, and some statistical data such as most used tags and most used policies. The Tagged Objects tag shows a list of all objects in your Snowflake instance, any tags that are assigned to them, and any policies that have been assigned.

Marketplace

The Marketplace page allows you to explore and search for published provider applications and datasets that are available to use in your Snowflake instance. There is a mixture of both free, freemium, and paid listings that you can explore and enable in your organization.

Activity

The Activity tab provides you with a few methods for exploring user activity within your Snowflake instance. This is probably the second-most used section in my Snowflake instance, especially working with the Snowflake SQL API, as it gives me a deeper insight into what activities my API calls are actually taking and rich detail regarding any errors I might encounter.

Query History

Query History allows you to view all of the queries executed in your Snowflake instance. A number of filters are provided to allow you to narrow down your inquiry, the most helpful being the User who executed a query, to make it easier to debug unexpected results in your API calls. The SQL Text will give you the exact SQL statement that executed in Snowflake, which can be helpful in understanding if the SQL you thought you passed via the API was actually received correctly by Snowflake, the Query ID to provide additional filtering if you have the ID from your API result, a Pass/Fail status, and the User who executed the query. Snowflake provides about ten columns you can configure to display on the screen based on the information you want to see.

If you drill into any one query activity, you'll see additional details regarding the query, including the full SQL Text and what results or response was returned by Snowflake for the query. The Query Profile tab is perhaps the most helpful element of Query History, giving you a full execution plan for your query. If a query is taking a long time to load results or is timing out based on your timeout settings, you can use this view to get a better understanding of what the query was doing and how long each function of the query took to run. Using these details, you can start to narrow down the elements of your query that could benefit from optimization to get better overall performance for the query.

Copy History

Copy History provides you with a detailed view of the COPY command in Snowflake. Using this information, you can see the progress of any data file you are copying into or out of your database, view past loads, and drill into individual load requests to learn more about the data entering your Snowflake instance and where it came from.

Task History

If you are leveraging Snowflake Tasks to run scheduled or manual queries, stored procedures, or functions, the Task History page gives you a breakdown of what tasks ran, when they ran, their run status, and other important metadata. Drilling into any Task will take you to its Run History page where you can see the past runs, their run result, and when the next task is scheduled to run (if you are using schedules).

Dynamic Tables

Dynamic tables allow you to materialize the results of a query that you specify, allowing you to bypass the need to create separate tables to handle transformation and data update functionality. Instead, you can define the target table as a dynamic table and specify the query statement that performs any transformations. Dynamic tables take on a refresh process to keep the data updated at regular intervals and replace the need for complete insert, update, and delete queries.

The Dynamic Tables tab allows you to see the Dynamic Tables you've created, their last refresh, and other valuable metadata that can help debug reasons why expected data is not appearing in your table.

Admin

In order to access the Admin tab, you must be granted the admin role within Snowflake. This tab allows you to manage various instances of your Snowflake instance. Because of that, it is recommended that you limit the number of users who have permissions to view these settings.

Usage

The Usage screen allows you to get a full breakdown of your Snowflake spend. You can use various filters to visualize your spend by warehouse, tags, users, services, and more. There are many spending tools available, both paid and free, that can leverage this data to give you deeper insights and optimization for your spend, such as Black Diamond (`https://blackdiamond360.com`).

It is a good idea to use this page or one of the various tools available to check your spending on, at minimum, a monthly basis to learn if you have errant queries or warehouses that are consuming a large number of credits and needlessly costing your organization money. As you get more familiar with the Snowflake SQL API and start leveraging it more heavily, this page is especially helpful in showing you if you are properly optimizing your API code and helping to identify areas where malicious users might be hitting your API and running up your credit consumption to no purpose.

Warehouses

When you first set up your Snowflake instance, you'll spend a decent amount of tab in the Warehouses section. A Snowflake warehouse is a cluster of computing resources for your Snowflake databases. These resources include CPU, memory allocation, and temporary storage. Snowflake uses t-shire sizing for warehouses (x-small, small, medium, large, etc.), and each size uses a different calculation to determine how many credits are consumed when it is running. In addition to warehouse sizing, you can also configure warehouse clustering. This facet of warehousing has an additional impact on your credit consumption. Because of the pricing model, it is important that you configure each warehouse based on its needs at the present. Warehouses can always be upgraded or downgraded, with no impact on downstream code, so err on the side of caution and know that less is more.

When configuring your warehouse, you need to consider the complexity of your query, the average amount of data your warehouse will be returning, and how often queries are being submitted to the warehouse. For complex queries or large datasets that take a long time to return, you'll want to increase your warehouse size. Larger warehouses can handle more complex SQL queries and return data faster than smaller queries. On the other hand, a larger warehouse does nothing to help a warehouse that receives a lot of concurrent SQL requests, big or small, as each warehouse has a concurrency limit that is determined by the size and complexity of each query. In such an instance, you'd want to enable warehouse clustering. This allows your warehouse to scale out additional nodes that can handle queries that might otherwise be queued.

When working with the Snowflake SQL API for Black Diamond, we took the approach of a single, shared Warehouse across. That is because we do not store customer data in our own Snowflake instance, and, with few exceptions, the complexity and number of concurrent requests we receive were a low risk that could be mitigated with a medium warehouse and a two-max clustering. Instead, upon creation of your account, a dedicated warehouse is created in your Snowflake instance that should be exclusively used by the Snowflake SQL API when Black Diamond requests are sent to your instance.

We created some additional statistics that pull details about your warehouse. Using this detail, our team can manually review accounts that are suffering from slow application speeds and take manual action to modify the warehouse used by the API to further optimize it. Additionally, automation within the tool can take some limited self-direction actions to mitigate performance issues while still working to keep the cost of credit consumption low.

Resource Monitors

If you have opted not to use a third-party tool for your Snowflake instance, Resource Monitors are a great way to keep an eye on credit consumption. You can assign Resource Monitors to one or all of your warehouses and specify a credit quote for each warehouse. This quota can be triggered to refresh on a daily, weekly, or monthly basis. Additionally, you can provide suspension settings that prevent a warehouse from exceeding its allocated usage. When you first start developing with the Snowflake SQL API, it is helpful to supply a low quota with a cutoff to prevent errant code from consuming a lot of credits when unsupervised and slowly increase that quota as your application grows and you become more comfortable with the API.

Users & Roles

We covered Users & Roles earlier in this chapter, but this section gives you insight into what users are allocated in your system, their last login, and what roles they have been granted. You can manage all aspects of a user from the Users tab, including creating and deleting users. The Roles tab allows you to do many of the same actions for roles within your organization. In addition, it provides a helpful mindmap view of your roles so you can quickly visualize how roles are laid out and how inheritance is set up for each role.

Security

The Security section allows you to define Network Policies for your organization and see what open sessions (users) are currently connected to Snowflake. Network Policies are a great way to further harden your Snowflake access by providing the ability to log in via certain IP addresses or blocking IP addresses that are particularly problematic. I recommend that all of your users be required to use multi-factor authentication (MFA), at a minimum, especially if they are not on an intranet or dedicated IP Address/IP Range where you can restrict access to just those addresses.

Since supporting multi-factor authentication is not possible through the API, it is highly recommended you create a Policy for your server's IP address(es) and assign it to your API user. In addition to the public/private key pair you created, this will provide an additional layer of security should your keys become compromised.

Billing & Terms

The Billing & Terms section provides you with a full detail of your Snowflake contract. It outlines what Terms of Service you have accepted and when, who your contacts are for billing, your payment methods, and a downloading version of all of your usage statements. Note that users who are on a prepaid capacity contract with Snowflake, allocating a lump sum of credits to their account, might not see a Payment Method listed.

Contacts

The Contacts page allows you to set what email(s) will receive notifications from Snowflake. Most important are the Security Notifications, which I recommend be assigned to someone who can regularly review these notifications and take action upon them. Privacy notifications keep you updated on the latest privacy policy changes or privacy concerns issued by Snowflake. In contrast, product notifications will keep you updated on Snowflake behavior changes, degraded performance, API changes, and other proactive notifications.

Accounts

Largely, you will not spend much time on the Accounts page unless you are in a large organization with specific data needs, including data localization and data governance policies. When you first sign up for Snowflake, a default account is created, which also acts as the organizational admin account for your Snowflake instance. If you find yourself needing additional accounts, you can create and manage these here.

One example of a reason you might use accounts would be if you service multiple customers and want to keep your customers' accounts segregated by account instead of databases and roles. This allows your customers to have more control over their data and access to their data without risking exposure to other customers you might service.

In another example, suppose you have data that has to stay within certain regions for governance reasons. A great use case would be educational data for Australia, which the government says cannot leave the confines of the country of Australia. You could easily set up a new account that lives on an Australian-based server and store all of your data specific to Australia there, thus satisfying the needs of the government regulation. You could also set up an account that takes a copy of your data from your main account and stores it on a server geographically located near a large group of your customers, allowing them to have much faster access to their data by not requiring them to have to submit a network request that has to travel half-way across the global to retrieve data.

Partner Connect

Partner Connect, similar to the Marketplace, allows you to connect directly to Snowflake partners who have built tools for Snowflake. One popular tool, DevOps for data, is DataOps.Live. This tool allows you to use DataOps and underlying DBT functionality to manage CI/CD pipelines for your Snowflake instance, giving you a truly agile data ingestion, modeling, and transformation process.

Because these partners have been built specifically for Partner Connect, you can quickly allow the necessary access to your Snowflake instance directly within the Partner Connect portal. This ensures you do not have to pass sensitive information to a third-party website, such as login details, which could become compromised if that system does not employ proper security standards.

As you leverage the Snowflake SQL API to build out your project, you might want to keep the Snowflake Partner Connect in mind. Not only does it provide a more secure way for you to allow your customers to connect your application to their Snowflake instance, but it also provides another advertisement channel by allowing you to be listed on the Partner Connect portal.

Accessing Snowflake SQL API

In this section, I will help you in getting started with accessing the Snowflake SQL API. As stated previously, the Snowflake SQL API is a REST API that you can use to access and update data in your Snowflake database. Using the API, you can execute standard SQL queries and most DDL and DML statements, as well as use the API to access metadata about your Snowflake instance from the Snowflake database. In this section, we will use Laravel 10 to show you how to connect to the Snowflake SQL API. This assumes you already have a base install of Laravel 10 up and running on a server or your local host, and are familiar with Laravel and PHP.

Creating A Snowflake Service

In order to ensure our code is DRY (Don't Repeat Yourself), navigate to *app* ➤ *Services* and create a new file called SnowflakeService.php. You'll want to include a few packages at the start of your file that will be necessary as we dive deeper.

Listing 3-1. Laravel Snowflake service

```
<?php

namespace App\Services;

use Carbon\Carbon;
```

```php
use Firebase\JWT\JWT;
use Firebase\JWT\Key;
use Illuminate\Http\Request;
use App\Http\Controllers\Controller
use Illuminate\Support\Facades\Auth;
use Illuminate\Support\Facades\Http;
use violuke\RsaSshKeyFingerprint\FingerprintGenerator;

class SnowflakeService
{
  // Future code here
}
```

The above code defines our namespace and some important packages, including the Firebase JWT package and the RsaSsheKeyFingerprint package by *violuke*. Now that you have your packages in place, we need to create the code that will allow you to get a JWT token, which will be used in your API call header. You'll want to generate a public and private key for your account. To do this, download the SnowSQL command-line package and then execute the following command:

First, generate an unencrypted version or an encrypted version

```
$ openssl genrsa 2048 | openssl pkcs8 -topk8 -inform PEM -out
rsa_key.p8 -nocrypt
```

or

```
$ openssl genrsa 2048 | openssl pkcs8 -topk8 -v2 des3 -inform
PEM -out rsa_key.p8
```

This command generates a private key in PEM format. Make sure it looks similar to the following:

```
-----BEGIN ENCRYPTED PRIVATE KEY-----
MIIE6TAbBgkqhkiG9w0BBQMwDgQILYPyCppzOwECAggABIIEyLiGSpeeGSe3xHP1
```

```
wHLjfCYycUPennlX2bd8yX8xOxGSGfvB+99+PmSlexOFmY9ov1J8H1H9Y3lMWXbL
...
-----END ENCRYPTED PRIVATE KEY-----
```

Once you have the private key, you'll need to generate a public key. Use the following command:

```
$ openssl rsa -in rsa_key.p8 -pubout -out rsa_key.pub
```

This command will create a file that should contain a similar format:

```
-----BEGIN PUBLIC KEY-----
MIIBIjANBgkqhkiG9w0BAQEFAAOCAQ8AMIIBCgKCAQEAy+Fw2q
v4Roud3l6tjPH4
zxybHjmZ5rhtCz9jppCV8UTWvEXxa88IGRIHbJ/PwKW/mR8L
XdfI7l/9vCMXX4mk
...
-----END PUBLIC KEY-----
```

Store both of these files in a secure, private directory on your local machine. When you are done, open a new SQL Worksheet in Snowflake, and assign the Public Key to your users:

```
ALTER USER johndoe SET RSA_PUBLIC_KEY='MIIBIjANBgkqh...';
```

Now that you have assigned the public key to your API user, we can start to construct the code needed for your JWT token generation. Go back to your Laravel code and open the SnowflakeService.php file we created earlier. Create a new function called generateJWT following the code below.

Listing 3-2. Laravel JTW generation

```
public static function generateJwt()
{
    $account = 'account identifier'
```

```
$username = 'snowflake_user_name'
$qualified_username = $account . '.' . $username;
$now = Carbon::now('UTC')->timestamp;
$lifetime =  Carbon::now('UTC')->addMinutes(59)->timestamp;

$public_key = 'Paste Public Key'
$private_key = 'Paste Private Key'

$fingerprint = FingerprintGenerator::getFingerprint($publ
ic_key, 'sha256');

$payload = [
    'iss' => $account . '.' . $username . '.SHA256:
    ' . $fingerprint,
    'sub' => $qualified_username,
    'iat' = $now
    'exp' = $lifetime
];

$jwt_token = JWT::encode($payload, $private_key, 'RS256');

return $jwt_token;
}
```

Let's take a moment to go through the above code. We start by defining our static function to generate the JWT token and specify a handful of variables that are needed for the token itself as well as the fingerprint. When I first started out using the Snowflake SQL API, I underestimated how important the fingerprint was; I was using a fingerprint generated by SnowSQL and assumed that was all that I needed because it "just worked" for around two weeks. When it stopped, it took a lot of debugging by reverse engineering the JWT token generated by the application vs. by SnowSQL to figure out how important the fingerprint is. There also was not a lot of good documentation on how to get this fingerprint using PHP or even Laravel, so I hope that this gives future users the jumpstart they need to do it correct the first time.

Once you have your fingerprint generated from the public key, and some other unique variables defined, we pass those to a payload array. The JWT encoding function accepts the array as its first argument, the private key as the second argument, and then we tell it to use RS256 for the encryption and validation. If you filled everything out correctly, you'll have a JWT token that can be used later in the SnowflakeService class, or you can print to screen and test it via the SnowSQL command-line.

The next section of code is small, but it was a helper method I created because I started working with multiple Snowflake accounts. The API URL actually changes with each Snowflake Account, not user, and is how you are able to specify your target instance to authenticate and execute against. Regardless as to whether you are accessing a single account or multiple accounts, I still recommend this helper function as it can be useful in other areas of your code as your application grows.

Listing 3-3. Laravel Snowflake base URL configuration

```
public static function createBaseURL($account, $region)
{
    $snowflake_api_base_url = 'https://' . $account . '.' .
    $region . '.snowflakecomputing.com';
    return $snowflake_api_base_url;
}
```

This function is pretty straightforward and generates the unique URL needed to specify where your code should direct the API call. We don't supply any of the REST functions, such as /api/v2/statements, because there are actually three functions we could call and we want that flexibility to append it on the fly. The next two functions we will look at are where the magic happens. The first is a basic execution function that handles a lot of upfront configuration of the API headers for most of your SQL statements, and the second function is how we handle partitioned data since the API returns "pages" of data that you must then requested in a paginated manner.

Listing 3-4. Laravel query execution

```
public static function execute($account, $region, $database,
$schema, $statement)
{
    $jwt = static::generateJwt();
    $base_url = static::createBaseURL($account, $region);

    $query = Http::withHeaders ([
        'Content-Type' => 'application/json',
        'User-Agent' => 'myApplication/1.0',
        'X-Snowflake-Authorization-Token-Type'
        => 'KEYPAIR_JWT',
    ])->acceptJson()->withToken($jwt)->post($base_url . '/api/
    v2/statements', [
        'statement' = $statement,
        'database' = $database,
        'warehouse' => 'warehouse_name',
        'schema' => $schema,
        'role' => 'role_name' // Can optionally be supplied as
        a function parameter
        'parameters' => [
            'query_tag' => 'my-application-name',
        ],
    ]);

    return $query;
}
```

Let's dissect this and explain what we are doing. We first define the execute function with some dynamic parameters we can supply and then generate both the JWT token and the base URL for the API. The magic really happens in the $query variable where we define the payload that gets sent using the Laravel HTTP package. In the headers, we are letting the API know

we are sending over a JSON body and telling Snowflake to expect a JWT key
pair for the authentication. Because we are using JWT, we need to supply
the withToken() method of the HTTP package, which automagically handles
passing the JWT token correctly to the API, and telling Snowflake we expect
a JSON response in return (an error, a success message, or the query results).
Within the post() method, we are defining the body as the SQL statement
we want to execute, the database and schema it should execute against,
the warehouse it should be using, and the user role to use. The parameter's
query tag is optional, but this is helpful when we are using the Query History
tab within Snowsight to filter down to the queries specifically sent by our API
for faster debugging or analysis.

Supposing we received a single page of query results and there are
multiple pages, or partitions, we can use the JSON response to grab the
statement handle and the next partition in the group and pass it to a helper
function specific to partition fetching.

Listing 3-5. Laravel Snowflake pagination

```
public static function getPartition($statementHandle,
$partition)
{
    $jwt = static::generateJwt();
    $base_url = static::createBaseUrl($account, $region);

    $query = Http::withHeaders([
        'Content-Type' => 'application/json',
        'User-Agent' => 'myApplication/1.0',
        'X-Snowflake-Authorization-Token-Type' =>
        'KEYPAIR_JWT',
    ])->acceptJson()->withToken($jwt)->get($base_url .
    '/api/v2/statements/' . $statementHandle .
```

```
    '?partition=' . $partition);

   return $query;
}
```

The above is very similar to our execute helper method but requires much less data. We are not actually passing any JSON body in this, or even making a POST call, but instead, we are making a GET call. This will go to the results we already generated in a previous call, directed by the statement handle, and return the results of the specified partition.

Now that you have a functional Laravel Service, the SnowflakeService class, you can include this class in your other code, such as Controllers, and quickly pass SQL queries via the API using the execute() method.

Things to Consider

We did not go over all of the security implications of this code, so let's take a moment to do so. First, it is not recommended you store your public and private key directly in code. You can opt to store it in a local database and salt the code, or you can install it in a 3rd party tool such as AWS Secrets Manager. Keeping your private key secure is very important to the security of your application. If you were following earlier in this chapter when we discussed Network Policies, your API user could further be restricted from being used either by the UI or the API by restricting its login to just the IP Address of your application server. If your private key were to then be compromised, the malicious user would need to then have access to your server to do anything meaningful with it. Because this key potentially has access to a lot of secure data, it is also recommended you not reuse a private key from any other system (such as your SSH key or your GitHub key).

The other risk that should be called out is that this could allow SQL injection into your Snowflake instance. After all, we are using Laravel to inject SQL code to Snowflake via the API, which is what we want, but we want to keep it from being maliciously used. One thing you could do is not allow any SQL to be passed directly to the execute function from a URL or form on your application. There are many ways to mitigate the risk, but I'll say the most important is to not allow your execute function to directly receive any SQL query that was directly generated by an end user via URL, form, or other method.

Last, you might consider lowering the JWT expiration token via the lifetime variable to something that is less than 59 minutes. This ensures that should someone perform a "man in the middle" attack on your server, they do not manage to grab the JWT token and use it elsewhere. Again, this is further mitigated if you are both keeping your private key secure and also implementing a Network Policy for the API user.

Conclusion

You should now have a solid understanding of the fundamentals of the Snowflake SQL API and the essential steps to get started. You have learned how to connect to Snowflake, navigate the environment, and perform basic data operations. With this foundational knowledge, you are well-equipped to delve deeper into the platform's more advanced features and functionalities. As you continue your journey, the skills acquired in this chapter will serve as a crucial stepping stone toward mastering Snowflake's powerful data management and analytics capabilities.

CHAPTER 4

SQL Basics in Snowflake Using Snowflake SQL API

In this chapter, we will review some of the fundamental functionality of SQL in the context of Snowflake and the Snowflake SQL API. The chapter talks in large part about common database and SQL concepts while introducing you to the specific nuances of Snowflake and the functionality and limitations of the SQL API. Within the landscape of data management and analytics, the mastery of fundamental SQL functions is akin to possessing the keys to a powerful kingdom. By providing the building blocks of SQL within Snowflake's dynamic ecosystem, this chapter will be a gateway to harnessing the full potential of Snowflake's SQL API, whether you are a novice navigating the data realm or an experienced practitioner seeking to refine your skills.

We will start by exploring the pivotal SELECT statement and its nuances for precise data retrieval and analysis. The subsequent focus on INSERT, UPDATE, and DELETE operations provides a strategic lens for shaping and maintaining datasets within your application, which is crucial for strategic data governance. We will then look at JOIN operations, which are critical for weaving intricate relationships between datasets.

© Ronald Steelman 2024
R. Steelman, *Mastering the Snowflake SQL API with Laravel 10,* Apress Pocket Guides,
https://doi.org/10.1007/979-8-8688-0382-6_4

We understand how JOIN criteria and WHERE clauses take a nuanced approach to conditional logic to empower professionals to extract targeted datasets, and follow it with aggregating and grouping data.

Key to ensuring we are executing performance-optimized querying, we will explore how subqueries and CTEs can be used within a single API call to quickly sort through and filter larger datasets before joining it to more refined data. This fundamental SQL technique is a key strategy we employ at Black Diamond to target queries that can be optimized, reduce compute costs for running warehouses, and cut down on remote and local spillage.

Finally, we will look at Snowflake's Bind Variable functionality. Bindings make it easier to work with dynamic filtering criteria and make it easier to handle the casting of data types. In addition to making for cleaner and easier-to-read code, it also cuts down on long SQL queries in your code, opting to pass this off to the Snowflake SQL API engine instead of handling this sometimes onerous task ourselves.

This chapter isn't just a tutorial; it's a strategic guide for professional developers and executives seeking to leverage Snowflake's SQL API for data mastery. As we navigate through the intricacies of these fundamental SQL functions, the ultimate goal is to empower you with the skills needed to orchestrate complex data operations and derive actionable insights for your application success.

SQL Fundamentals: SELECT, INSERT, UPDATE, and DELETE

In this section, we delve into the core fundamentals of SQL, focusing on the four foundational operations: SELECT, INSERT, UPDATE, and DELETE. As the backbone of data exploration and manipulation, these operations play a crucial role in shaping and extracting insights from datasets.

SELECT Statements

The SELECT statement for data retrieval and analysis. Here, we dissect its nuances, exploring how to craft precise queries that unveil valuable insights. We will cover the spectrum of the SELECT clause, empowering you to navigate and interpret vast datasets effectively. The SELECT statement resides at the heart of any data-centric operation and is a commonly used tool in the arsenal of every data professional. The versatility of the SELECT statement makes our objective clear in the context of your application: to empower you with the skill needed to navigate and interpret vast datasets effectively, whether you're dealing with millions or just a few, and handing that data off to your application for further processing.

Why do I start with the SELECT statement? The SELECT statement is the most commonly executed SQL statement. At least 75% of the queries you'll execute using the Snowflake SQL API are using the SELECT clause. Beyond that, understanding how the SELECT clause works, especially in defining column sets to be queried, will make it easier for you to work with the returned data result set. To start, let's look at the technical definition of the SELECT statement for Snowflake.

Listing 4-1. Snowflake SELECT statement dictionary

```
SELECT [ { ALL | DISTINCT } ]
      [ TOP <n> ]
      [{<object_name> | <alias>} . ]*

      [ ILIKE '<pattern>' ]

      [ EXCLUDE
         {
             <col_name> | ( <col_name>, <col_name>, . . . )
         }
      ]
```

```
[ REPLACE
    {
        ( <expr> AS <col_name> [ , <expr> AS <col_name>,
        . . . ] )
    }
]
[ RENAME
    {
        <col_name> AS <col_alias>
        | ( <col_name> AS <col_alias>, <col_name> AS
        <col_alias>, . . . )
    }
]
```

This may seem complex at first, and that is understandable, especially if you are new to SQL and have had little or no exposure to syntax definition formatting used by most database providers to explain how a particular SQL function works. The first line tells the query processing engine we are executing a SELECT clause and specifies what records we want to return. By default, the engine assumes the ALL, which returns all records in the dataset and does not need to be specified if that is your goal. The DISTINCT keyword will eliminate duplicate values from your result set. Both of these are executed using standard order of operations. By this, I mean that any WHERE clauses and JOIN statements will be honored first, and then the result set will be further filtered if you have specified the DISTINCT keyword. In our query window, we would write this like *SELECT DISTINCT * * or *SELECT *.

The following keyword in the structure is the TOP <n> keyword. In older database systems, there was a distinct use case for using the TOP <n> keyword in your queries. Snowflake included it, as do many other database solutions, to provide cross-platform support for your queries from other systems. However, this keyword supports the same functionality as the LIMIT clause, and Snowflake considers them equivalent with no differences. Like the LIMIT clause, this limits the number of rows returned in the result set. Following the order of operations, your result set will be filtered based on your WHERE and JOIN statements, among other clauses we'll explore later, whether or not you used the DISTINCT keyword, and then return the final result set within the specific limit. For example, executing *SELECT TOP 100 ** in your query window will only return 100 records in the result set. Without the use of ORDER BY clauses or other query syntax, the 100 records to use are entirely determined by the query processing engine and could vary with each execution. Outside of this basic functionality, it is essential to know that if you are leveraging the OFFSET clause in your SQL statement, the OFFSET clause requires you to use LIMIT and does not support TOP.

Moving forward, the <object_name> or <alias> is a way to identify the object or alias defined in the FROM clause. If you are joining multiple tables of data together, you will need a way to reference columns in each dataset. This might limit the number of columns being returned, control the order of the columns returned, or provide a way to distinguish between more than one column with the same name across multiple datasets.

Last, the ILIKE, EXCLUDE, REPLACE, and RENAME keywords provide ways to manipulate the columns further returned, not the data itself, when working with specific columns. ILIKE will look for column names that match the pattern and return only those columns, allowing you to quickly pull a subset of columns from a wide table that meets the pattern criteria. Similarly, if you are working with a very wide table and need to return all columns except a few, it is easier to use the EXCLUDE keyword to leave those few columns out instead of specifying the larger majority of the columns you do want to return. Finally, REPLACE and RENAME offer very similar functionality in changing the column's name. Where RENAME simply changes the column from what is in the table to the name you specify (changing AVG_COST_ACCR to AVERAGE_COST_ACCURED), the REPLACE keyword accepts an expression to do dynamic renaming (e.g., replacing an underscore in column names with a dash).

Now, why is all of this important? Well, apart from providing you with the tools you need to reference column names in a format that you understand quickly or to select specific columns when joining across multiple tables or datasets, these keywords give you the tools to do two things: ensure you are executing optimized queries and not requiring you to know the exact structure of your tables or the structure of returned datasets (especially when joining across multiple datasets).

In the case of the former, it is a bad form or practice to execute a SELECT query with the asterisks (*) symbol. That is because the asterisks will return all columns in whatever order they appear in the table structure, and we don't always need all of the data for these columns. This can greatly increase compute time, the time it takes to return the dataset back across the API, and can have other performance impacts.

In the latter example, if you are required to know the exact format of the table structure, it makes retrieving specific data in the API result set much harder to predict. This increases by multiples when you are joining multiple sets of data together, and you have to anticipate how all those columns are given an ordinal position in the resulting JSON response. Let's look at some real examples to illustrate what I mean. Take the following API call.

Listing 4-2. Laravel REST API handler—SELECT all columns

```
$query = Http::withHeaders([
    'Content-Type' => 'application/json',
    'User-Agent' => 'myApplication/1.0',
    'X-Snowflake-Authorization-Token-Type' => 'KEYPAIR_JWT',
])->acceptJson()->withToken($jwt)->post($snowflake_api_base_
url.'/api/v2/statements', [
    'statement' => "SELECT * FROM customers;",
    'database' => $database,
    'warehouse' => $connection->warehouse,
    'schema' => $schema,
```

```
    'role' => $connection->role,
    'parameters' => [
      'query_tag' => 'black-diamond',
    ],
  ]);
```

Specifically, we are focusing on the underlined JSON key. You can see that we are executing a SELECT query against the customers' table and telling the query processing engine to return all columns for that table. Now, if you do not know the exact structure of that table, you are not going to be able to easily pull the data you want for each row returned in the result set. Here is an example of a result set returned by the API.

Listing 4-3. Laravel API result response

```
{
  "code": "090001",
  "statementHandle": "536fad38-b564-4dc5-9892-a4543504df6c",
  "sqlState": "00000",
  "message": "successfully executed",
  "createdOn": 1597090533987,
  "statementStatusUrl": "/api/v2/statements/536fad38-
  b564-4dc5-9892-a4543504df6c",
  "resultSetMetaData" : {
  "rowType": [
   {
     "name":"ROWNUM",
     "type":"FIXED",
     "length":0,
     "precision":38,
     "scale":0,
     "nullable":false
   }, {
```

```
    "name":"ACCOUNT_NAME",
    "type":"TEXT",
    "length":1024,
    "precision":0,
    "scale":0,
    "nullable":false
  }, [. . .]
    "numRows" : 50000,
    "format" : "jsonv2",
    "partitionInfo" : [ {
      "rowCount" : 12288,
      "uncompressedSize" : 124067,
      "compressedSize" : 29591
    }, {
      "rowCount" : 37712,
      "uncompressedSize" : 414841,
      "compressedSize" : 84469
    }],
  },
  "data": [
    ["customer1", "1234 A Avenue", "98765", "2021-01-20
    12:34:56.03459878"],
    ["customer2", "987 B Street", "98765", "2020-05-31
    01:15:43.765432134"],
    ["customer3", "8777 C Blvd", "98765", "2019-07-01
    23:12:55.123467865"],
    ["customer4", "64646 D Circle", "98765", "2021-08-03
    13:43:23.0"]
  ]
}
```

Notice that the response key we care most about is the **data** key. Using this key, we can loop over every row and pull out the data using something like:

```
$row0 = $query_result['data'][0];
$row1 = $query_result['data'][1];
```

But what if we want a specific column, such as the CREATED_ ON column, at the end of each row of data? If we did not know the exact structure of the table, we'd have to first loop through the [resultSetMetaData][rowType][name] keys to get the ordinal key and the value. In this example, that would be the fifth key (or ordinal key four since this behaves like an array). Your application code can start to get very messy and complex with all of that looping just to find out you need to do the following:

```
$row0_created = $query_result['data'][0][4];
$row1_created = $query_result['data'][1][4];
```

Instead, we should define our columns in the SELECT statement. This gives us the advantage of optimizing our query by not pulling data we do not plan to use but also gives us control of the ordinal key position of each column. Observe the following code refactored from before.

Listing 4-4. Laravel REST API handler with column specification

```
$query = Http::withHeaders([
    'Content-Type' => 'application/json',
    'User-Agent' => 'myApplication/1.0',
    'X-Snowflake-Authorization-Token-Type' => 'KEYPAIR_JWT',
  ])->acceptJson()->withToken($jwt)->post($snowflake_api_base_
  url.'/api/v2/statements', [
```

```
    'statement' => "SELECT CREATED_ON, ADDRESS, ZIP FROM
    customers;",
    'database' => $database,
    'warehouse' => $connection->warehouse,
    'schema' => $schema,
    'role' => $connection->role,
    'parameters' => [
      'query_tag' => 'black-diamond',
    ],
  ]);
```

Because we have defined the columns in the SELECT statement, and in the order that we want them, we can now predict with a high level of accuracy the ordinal key needed to access a specific column. Now our code looks something like this:

```
$row0_address = $query_result['data'][0][1];
$row1_address= $query_result['data'][1][1];
```

The reason we can do this is because we know that the columns are being returned in the order they were specified in the SELECT statement (0 => CREATED_ON, 1=> ADDRESS, 2 => ZIP). In this example, we eliminate the need for you to know the table structure beforehand or rely on your application to derive the correct key. If we had to rely on our knowledge of the table, we would introduce bad data to our application if a developer added a new column in the middle of the table. Suppose we rely on our application to derive the key. In that case, you are writing a lot of unnecessary code to loop through the result metadata to find the ordinal keys each time, adding both development time overhead and application execution overhead.

INSERT Statements

From time to time, you might need to insert new data into your Snowflake instance. This could be data generated by your application, data received by user input, or data your application processes from third parties that then must be persisted to your database. Because of the nature of the application my team and I built around the Snowflake SQL API, that being a multi-tenant solution for Snowflake observability and performance, we only rarely insert data to the database using the API. That is because the data that drives our tool lives in our internal instance of Snowflake, which we use a PHP Driver to interact with, but there are times we have to create data in a customers' instance within the application database that gets created on each install. Inserting data into Snowflake uses the INSERT clause with the following syntax.

Listing 4-5. Snowflake INSERT statement dictionary

```
INSERT [ OVERWRITE ] INTO <target_table> [ ( <target_col_name>
[ , ... ] ) ]
    {
      VALUES ( { <value> | DEFAULT | NULL } [ , ... ] ) [ , (
      ... ) ] |
      <query>
    }
```

The syntax here is much more straightforward than what we saw with the SELECT clause. You have the ability to insert new data, or optionally overwrite existing data, using the INSERT clause and specifying the column names and the values, or data, for each record. The API does allow you to insert multiple rows of data, but this adds some complexities to your code that we'll talk about below. One thing to note: the OVERWRITE keyword does not behave like an "upsert" of data. Instead, this is a quick way to truncate all of the existing data in a table and replace it with the new data without having to specify multiple queries.

51

When it comes to inserting data, inserting single records of data is fairly straightforward. In your SQL statement, you'll want to specify the column names and then supply variables of your data as the values so that, in this way, you can construct a dynamic insert statement. Where this could get complex is in an instance where you have a lot of columns that need to be populated or if you are performing multi-insert operations. Snowflake, albeit inadvertently, does provide a clean solution for this.

Touching briefly upon a more advanced topic, Snowflake, like most all database solutions, provides the ability to create Stored Procedures. You can create these directly in Snowflake, using the SnowSQL command line tool, or by having your application run a one-time configuration script via the API. For example, my application expects various Stored Procedures to exist in a customers' Snowflake instance in order to run properly. When a customer sets up a new connection for the first time, they are prompted to run a "Deploy Configuration" script.

This script uses the API to create the various objects, tasks, and stored procedures in their Snowflake instance. We version this configuration and store it in the connections table in a column called "config_version_deployed". If this value is NULL or set to a version lower than the current version, the user will be displayed a banner prompting them to run the new or latest configuration. Because we must do this via the API to take manual effort off of the customer, the configuration script does get somewhat long and complex. However, the trade-off is cleaner code within the rest of the application and was felt to be an overall solid solution.

Why is this important to know? In an instance where we have to insert multiple records to a table, we have constructed a Stored Procedure for that table to handle the INSERT of data. The body of the function is our SQL statement set up in a loop. The function accepts three parameters: the table name, an array of the column names, and an array of the values. Because we have coded this into our application to be handled the same way each time, we can ensure that the first-level array keys for the values match the ordinal key of the columns, and from there, we are able to dynamically construct the INSERT query within the Stored Procedure.

One thing to note here is that we created a procedure that allows us to dynamically handle any table insert we are working with. This cut down on the number of procedures we had to make—one dynamic procedure instead of a procedure for each table we would insert data into. This allows us to follow the DRY method (Don't Repeat Yourself), results in having to run fewer configuration upgrades which could consume more credits for our customers, and overall was the design pattern we chose to follow. You might have a use case where you want or need to have each table handled by its own function, and that is 100% fine to do. There is no right or wrong way to handle this.

UPDATE Statements

The UPDATE clause works in a similar fashion to the INSERT clause and gives you the ability to update an existing record, or multiple records, in a database. There will be many instances that you need to update data, ranging from very simple to highly complex, and the statement is flexible enough to handle these. Suppose for a moment you need to track when a user last logged into the system. A very simple UPDATE query can set the "last_login_timestamp" to the current date/time, which gets executed each time the user processes a login request on the application. A more complex example might be if your application performs various data calculations, either on user demand or in the background, and needs to persist that data to the database. We can see below the syntax, being fairly straightforward, for the UPDATE clause.

Listing 4-6. Snowflake UPDATE statement dictionary

```
UPDATE <target_table>
       SET <col_name> = <value> [ , <col_name> =
       <value> , ... ]
         [ FROM <additional_tables> ]
         [ WHERE <condition> ]
```

Because of the simplicity of the UPDATE statement, you might be deceived into thinking that your application code will be just as simple. While this may be true for many of your requirements, we again must look back to how quickly the query can grow into a large demand on your application code. Similar to the INSERT statement, having an UPDATE statement with a large column set, or even having a column that supports unstructured data, the UPDATE query can quickly grow and create a lot of technical debt.

If your query has fewer than five columns and does not require handling unstructured data, you can consider it a good rule of thumb that you can create the query directly within the API call. If, however, your query does not follow this pattern, or you simply want to have cleaner code, you can choose to create a dynamic Stored Procedure like we did for inserting data. One thing to keep in mind is that it is very important that you supply at least one WHERE condition, as should always be the case when doing an UPDATE in SQL, to prevent you from erroneously overwriting good data. Because of the need to supply these conditions, if you are choosing to create a Stored Procedure to be called by your code via the API, you would need to have a parameter that supports an array of where conditions that can be dynamically loaded into the query.

DELETE Statements

The last of the four foundational SQL clauses is the DELETE clause. Unlike the TRUNCATE clause, which empties all of the data from a table, the DELETE clause allows you to specify WHERE conditions to selectively delete data and even allows you to specify additional tables or queries to support your WHERE conditions. The syntax for this clause is the most simple of the four, but within the simplicity is the flexibility to be a very powerful query.

Listing 4-7. Snowflake DELETE statement dictionary

```
DELETE FROM <table_name>
          [ USING <additional_table_or_query> [, <additional_
          table_or_query> ] ]
          [ WHERE <condition> ]
```

When working with the DELETE clause, it is vital you supply at least one WHERE condition to prevent you from deleting all of your data. If your intent is to truly wipe the table clean, it is recommended you use the TRUNCATE clause as it is faster. Where the DELETE clause must evaluate every record before deleting it, even if there are no WHERE conditions supplied, the TRUNCATE clause simply empties the table without evaluating any of the records beforehand.

In our application, and as a best practice that we follow, we do not delete data from the database. Instead, we employ an "is_deleted" flag that indicates a record should no longer be used but allows us to retain the data. This may not be a viable approach for your application due to various reasons, but if one of those reasons is storage capacity, it is good to note that storage has come a long way over the years and is fairly cheap at a large scale.

55

Instances where you might choose to delete data directly from a table instead of supplying your version of an "is_deleted" flag might include: following governmental compliance such as GDRP, removing bad data, or purging sensitive customer data that should not be kept for long periods of time or after the customer has churned.

If you anticipate having to perform data deletions via the SQL API, you can usually get away with constructing these queries in real time within your application code. If, however, you are dealing with complex WHERE conditions, especially involving the use of other tables or queries to refine the targeted data to be deleted, you might opt for a more dynamic approach using a Stored Procedure. Again, the two things to keep in mind are keeping your code from growing so large it is hard to manage and following a DRY approach to your application development.

JOIN Operations and WHERE Clauses

Now that we have covered the four foundational query clauses, we will dive into joins and filtering clauses. These two subjects have been grouped together because a table join supplies additional data to your query results and has the added functionality of filtering data. Like most database systems, Snowflake supports the four common join types: inner joins, outer joins, cross joins, and natural joins.

As I stated, joins can have the added functionality of filtering your data, whether through the nature of the join itself or by supplying join criteria that act as a filter on the data being joined. One of these is the inner join. With an inner join, each row in a table matches a row in another table. When a row in one table does not match the row in another table, those rows are excluded from the query result. Take a situation where you have students at a university and an active student is considered any student enrolled in at least one class. By joining students to class enrollments on a key such as a student_id, you would only get classes that have students in them and, similarly, only get students who had an associated class. If you were to take this result and further filter it using a SELECT DISTINCT clause on student_id, first_name, and last_name, you would get a unique list of students who are active at the university. We do this to account for students enrolled in multiple classes, which would create duplicate student records in the result set by the nature of an inner join.

Let us explore the various JOINs in Snowflake.

Natural Join or Join

Using the *NATURAL JOIN* clause, or *JOIN* for short, you can join two tables containing columns with identical names and corresponding data. Continuing with our example of a university, we might have a table called **enrolled_classes** and **class_grades**. Both of these tables would have a column called **student_id** so that a student can be linked to their enrolled class, and a student can be linked to their class grade.

Because both tables have a column called **student_id**, the join will automatically construct the ON clause and join on those two columns. This means you do not have to write the ON criteria: *[NATURAL] JOIN on enrolled_classes.student_id = class_grades.student_id*. The nature of the join already assumes you want to join those two columns and handles it for you. If both tables have multiple matching columns, the natural join will automatically join on all of those columns.

The natural join will only include one record for shared columns and will omit the other records. Natural joins can be combined with an outer join, and you can specify criteria for filtering in the WHERE clause, but you cannot specify custom ON clause criteria.

LEFT OUTER JOIN

A left outer join includes all rows in the primary table, even if there are rows that do not match, and any matching rows in the joined table. The primary table, or the "left table," is the table specified in the FROM clause. The joined table, or the "right table," is the one specified in the join clause. For example, using our university example we might have the following query:

```
SELECT s.full_name, s.student_id, c.class_name FROM students s
        LEFT OUTER JOIN enrolled_classes ec ON ec.student_
        id = s.student_id
```

In this example, we would get a list of all students and their student ID, and the class name of any class they are enrolled in as indicated by the matching criteria in the ON clause. We could further filter this down to show just students who are enrolled in a class by supplying a WHERE clause like: *WHERE c.class_name IS NOT NULL.* If we wanted to show students who are not enrolled in a class, we would do so as follows: *WHERE c.class_name IS NULL.*

RIGHT OUTER JOIN

A right outer join includes all rows in the joined table, or the "right table", and any matching rows in the primary table (or the "left table").

```
SELECT s.full_name, s.student_id, c.class_name FROM students s
        RIGHT OUTER JOIN enrolled_classes ec ON ec.student_
        id = s.student_id
```

In this example, we would get a list of all rows in class_name values in the enrolled_classes table, as well as the full_name and student_id values for any matching records as specified in the ON clause.

FULL OUTER JOIN

A full outer join will include all rows from both tables, regardless of the ON criteria, giving you a full dataset as if the rows all lived in a single table. Rows that match will be returned as a single row and unmatched rows will

all return as their own row. Any unmatched students will have no class_
name value, and any unmatched enrolled_classes will have no full_name
or student_id values.

```
SELECT s.full_name, s.student_id, c.class_name FROM students s
        FULL OUTER JOIN enrolled_classes ec ON ec.student_
        id = s.student_id
```

INNER JOIN

In our example of a left outer join, we described how you can use a WHERE
clause to filter out unmatched rows. A shorter way to write this, and a
more optimized way, is to use an inner join. When you use an inner join,
it returns only those rows for which there is a match based on your ON
criteria.

```
SELECT s.full_name, s.student_id, c.class_name FROM students s
        INNER JOIN enrolled_classes ec ON ec.student_id =
        s.student_id
```

In this example, only rows where there is a match of student_id will be
returned. Therefore, you'll always have values for full_name, student_id,
and class_name. Since it is possible that a student could be enrolled in
multiple classes, you can expect that the full_name and student_id record
will be duplicated for each class the student is enrolled in.

CROSS JOIN

Finally, we have a cross join. This join takes both tables and returns every
possible combination of rows (sometimes referred to as a "Cartesian
product" or "Cartesian join"). This means that most of the rows will
contain parts of rows that are not actually related, which can render a cross
join useless in many instances.

Using a cross join can cause your returned dataset to become very large, resulting in a more expensive query execution plan. When the first table has N number of rows and the second table has Z number of rows, the result would be a product of the two (N x Z). This means that the first table having 100 rows and the second table having 100 rows would result in a dataset containing 100,000 rows.

A final thing to note is that, like the natural join, the cross join does not support an ON clause. That is because all possible joins are honored, rendering the use of the ON clause useless by nature.

Aggregating, Grouping, and Ordering Data

Now that we have a good understanding of how to join data across multiple tables, let's take a look at how we can refine and give order to chaos on that data. We will look at a few aggregate functions, grouping functions, and ordering of data. Because these functions are so vast and versatile, especially with the aggregate functions, we will not cover them all in this material. Instead, this is meant to be an introduction to how you can further refine and organize your data to make more sense of the results.

GROUP BY

We will first look at the GROUP BY clause, as it is important in supporting aggregate functions. The GROUP BY clause groups rows with the same group-by-item expression and computes aggregate functions for the resulting group. You can specify multiple items in the grouping to further refine your results. Let's look at an example:

```
SELECT  cv.student_id FROM campus_violations cv
GROUP BY cv.student_id
```

This query will group both values and return a single row for each unique grouping. If a student has multiple violations on campus, it will only return the student_id one time. This method might be used to determine which students have ever had a campus violation since being at the school.

```
SELECT  cv.student_id, cv.type FROM campus_violations cv
GROUP BY cv.student_id, cv.type
```

Taking it one step further, we can group by type. If a student has had multiple violations of type "parking" you would get a single record with their student_id and the type of parking. If the student has other violation types, each type will return a single record of that student_id and the type of violation they had, resulting in seeing a record for the student_id multiple times for each type.

```
SELECT  cv.student_id, cv.type FROM campus_violations cv
GROUP BY cv.student_id, cv.type
HAVING COUNT(cv.student_id) > 1
```

From here, perhaps we want to only see students who are repeat offenders. Here we are further refining the query by telling it to only give us a student_id and their associated violation type if they have had more than one violation on campus. If a student_id appears in the table only one time, it will not be returned. The HAVING clause allows you to define general expressions that can evaluate how the GROUP BY returns data.

```
SELECT  cv.student_id, cv.type, COUNT(cv.full_name) AS
violation_count FROM campus_violations cv
GROUP BY cv.student_id, cv.type
HAVING COUNT(cv.student_id) > 1
```

Finally, we can get an idea of how many violations a student has had of each type by supplying the aggregate function of COUNT in the SELECT clause. If a student had six parking violations, you'd see a record result with the student_id, the type of parking, and a value of 6.

It is important to note that when you use a GROUP BY clause, you must either match your SELECT clause so that any column appearing in the SELECT clause also appears in the GROUP BY clause or you must wrap unmatched columns in an aggregate function. In the previous example, you'll notice that full_name is wrapped in the COUNT aggregate function, but full_name does not appear in the GROUP BY clause. That is because, by nature, the aggregate function already groups data together.

Aggregate Functions

Aggregate functions are means of transforming your data so that they can be used for more meaningful exploration. You might use the AVG function to get an average of all values, the SUM function to get a summation of all values, the MIN function to get the lowest value, and so on. Let's go back to our university example and look at an example query:

```
SELECT s.full_name, s.student_id, g.grade FROM students s
            INNER JOIN grades g ON g.student_id = s.student_id
```

This example will return all students and a list of their grades. Since a student could have multiple grades, depending on if they are enrolled in multiple classes, you will see the full_name and student_id repeated multiple times. We can take this query one step further and define a grade-point average for the student:

```
SELECT s.full_name, s.student_id, AVG(g.grade) AS grade_average
FROM students s
            INNER JOIN grades g ON g.student_id = s.student_id
GROUP BY s.full_name, s.student_id
```

This example introduces our first aggregate function, the average function (AVG), and defines the column name (*AS grade_average*). If we did not define a column name, the result set would return the column name as **AVG(g.grade)**. The returned list will give you a unique list of full_name and student_id values, and the average of all of the grade values for the matching records. If we wanted to know what the lowest grade each student received is, we could add *MIN(g.grade)* to the query and it would return the lost grade in the list of grades for that student.

Ordering Data

Finally, let us look at how to order data. When you return your dataset, you might need it to output in a specific ordering of information. Perhaps you want all student_ids to appear together or you want the most recent version of each record first. When you use an ORDER BY clause, you can specify how the data gets returned.

```
SELECT s.full_name, s.student_id, s.enrolled_date FROM students s
ORDER BY s.enrolled_date DESC
```

In this example, we are returning a list of all students who have ever enrolled at the university. The ORDER BY clause says to take the enrolled_date and order it in descending order. The resulting set would return the most recently enrolled student and then continue backwards in time. If you were instead to change the *DESC* flag to *ASC*, it would return the oldest student, presumably the student who enrolled first at the university, and then continue forward in time. You can also specify more than one ORDER BY criteria for sorting.

```
SELECT s.full_name, s.student_id, s.enrolled_date, s.last_seen_
date FROM students s
ORDER BY s.last_seen_date DESC, s.enrolled_date DESC
```

In this example, we would get a list of all students who ever enrolled at the university. You'd see them first in the order of when they were last seen in the university systems. If multiple students had the same last_seen date, say the start of a new semester, it would then sort it further by the student who enrolled most recently.

It is important to know that without an ORDER BY clause, the results returned by a query are an unordered set. This means if you run the same query repeatedly, the resulting output could be sorted differently each time it is run. If order matters, or if you want a greater chance of reusing cached data from a previous run of the query, you should leverage the ORDER BY clause.

Subqueries and CTEs

Subqueries and CTEs are a way of making queries more performant by filtering down initial datasets before, as an example, joining the data to other tables. Imagine that your university has over one million students in the database and has had over five million enrolled class entries. This assumes that you only had five classes and each student enrolled in each of those classes. As we know, a university probably has more than five classes, classes can be considered a different class if it is for a different semester, and you probably have multiple students enrolled in each class. The data can quickly begin to compound and cause your query to run slow or even time out. In the world of Snowflake, this can be very expensive as the Warehouse must stay running longer and consume more credits. So, how do we fix this? One way is through the use of a subquery.

```
SELECT s.full_name, s.student_id, ec.class_name, ec.class_code
FROM students s
INNER JOIN enrolled_classes ec ON ec.student_id = s.student_id
ORDER BY s.student_id ASC
```

This query will return all students, in the order of the smallest student_id first, and any class they have ever been enrolled in. This potentially is a lot of data. If we want to filter down the number of students, we could use a WHERE clause, but perhaps the data we need for the filter lives in yet another table. A subquery can fix this:

```
SELECT s.full_name, s.student_id, ec.class_name, ec.class_code
FROM (
    SELECT sqs.full_name, sqs.student_id FROM students sqs
    INNER JOIN class_grades sqcg ON sqcg.student_id = sqs.
    student_id
    WHERE AVG(sqcg.grade) < 72
) s
INNER JOIN enrolled_classes ec ON ec.student_id = s.student_id
ORDER BY s.student_id ASC
```

The above example will first run the query inside the FROM clause and return a list of student_name and student_id values for all students who have an average grade point below 72%. We consider these students to be at risk of flunking out or losing financial aid due to a low GPA. Once we have this sub-set of students, we return those students with their class name and class code. I still think we can filter this further.

```
SELECT s.full_name, s.student_id, ec.class_name, ec.class_code
FROM (
    SELECT sqs.full_name, sqs.student_id FROM students sqs
    INNER JOIN class_grades sqcg ON sqcg.student_id = sqs.
    student_id
    WHERE AVG(sqcg.grade) < 72
) s
INNER JOIN (
    SELECT sqec.class_name, sqec.class_code FROM enrolled_
    classes sqec
    INNER JOIN class_semesters sqcs ON sqec.class_code = sqcs.
    class_code
    WHERE sqcs.semester_name = 'Fall' AND sqcs.semester_year
    = '2023'
)ec ON ec.student_id = s.student_id
ORDER BY s.student_id ASC
```

This query will first get the previous list of students based on the first subquery we already looked at. The second subquery will then evaluate and return only classes that happened in Fall of the 2023 semester. Once both subqueries evaluate, the resulting data will be joined, any unmatched data will filter out because of the inner join, and a much more manageable set of data will be returned.

Working with Bind Variables

Getting back into the topic of the Snowflake SQL API, the use of bind variables makes it easier to have cleaner and more dynamic code. Let's look at an example of a bind variable in the context of the API.

Listing 4-8. Laravel API handler with bind variables

```
$query = Http::withHeaders([
        'Content-Type' => 'application/json',
        'User-Agent' => 'myApplication/1.0',
        'X-Snowflake-Authorization-Token-Type' =>
        'KEYPAIR_JWT',
    ])->acceptJson()->withToken($jwt)->post($snowflake_api_
    base_url.'/api/v2/statements', [
        'statement' => "SELECT CREATED_ON, ADDRESS, ZIP
        FROM customers WHERE LAST_ORDER_DATE BETWEEN ?
        AND ?;",
        'database' => $database,
        'warehouse' => $connection->warehouse,
        'schema' => $schema,
        'role' => $connection->role,
        'parameters' => [
            'query_tag' => 'black-diamond',
        ],
```

```
'bindings': {
    '1': {
        'type': 'TEXT',
        'value': '2023-10-01'
    },
    '2': {
        'type': 'TEXT',
        'value': '2023-12-31'
    },
  },
]);
```

The query above uses a BETWEEN function in the statement to find all customers who have an order between a specific set of dates. We use two question marks (?) to denote where we should bind variables. The first question mark will have a binding of 1, the second a binding of 2, and so on in the order that they appear.

If you were to change the value of both bindings out for a dynamic code such as $quarterstartdate and $quarterenddate, you could then have your code specify the start and end date of a quarter based on some form of earlier coding logic. By moving the code into the bindings, it means that the statement section looks cleaner, overall, and makes for an all-around cleaner block of code. In addition, there is a security advantage to using bind variables. Through the use of a bind variable, you can prevent SQL injection attacks from man-in-the-middle attacks or from user input.

CHAPTER 5

Advanced SQL Techniques Using Snowflake SQL API

In this chapter, we will transcend the boundaries of conventional data querying and dive into the depths of sophisticated data manipulation. In this chapter, we embark on a journey that elevates your SQL proficiency to new heights, equipping you with the tools and techniques to tackle complex data challenges confidently and precisely.

Data Transformation with CASE and COALESCE

The CASE statement is a powerful tool in the arsenal of SQL developers, offering a versatile mechanism for conditional logic and value transformation within queries. In this section, we delve into the intricacies of the CASE statement, uncovering its myriad applications and demonstrating how it can elevate the sophistication of your SQL queries.

At its core, the CASE statement provides a flexible means of implementing conditional logic within SQL queries, allowing developers to perform different actions based on specified conditions. Whether you need to categorize data, calculate derived values, or customize query outputs, the CASE statement offers a concise and intuitive syntax for achieving

© Ronald Steelman 2024
R. Steelman, *Mastering the Snowflake SQL API with Laravel 10*, Apress Pocket Guides,
https://doi.org/10.1007/979-8-8688-0382-6_5

these objectives. By mastering the nuances of the CASE statement, you'll unlock a world of possibilities for data manipulation and analysis within Snowflake's dynamic ecosystem.

Beyond its basic functionality, the CASE statement excels in handling complex business logic and transforming data dynamically. Support for multiple conditions and nested CASE expressions empowers developers to address a wide range of scenarios with precision and efficiency. From data cleansing and standardization to advanced reporting and decision-making, the CASE statement serves as a cornerstone for driving actionable insights and enhancing the value of your SQL queries. Below is an example of a CASE query.

Listing 5-1. Snowflake CASE query

```sql
SELECT
    s.full_name
  , s.student_id
  ,CASE
      WHEN  ec.class_code LIKE 'MATH%' THEN 'Mathematics'
      WHEN  ec.class_code LIKE 'SCI%' THEN 'Sciences'
      WHEN  ec.class_code LIKE 'PSY%' THEN 'Psychologies'
    ELSE ec.class_code
  ,CASE
      WHEN  RIGHT(ec.class_code, 1) = 1 THEN '1 Credit'
      WHEN  RIGHT(ec.class_code, 1)  = 2 THEN '2 Credits'
      WHEN  RIGHT(ec.class_code, 1)  = 3 THEN '3 Credits'
      WHEN  RIGHT(ec.class_code, 1)  = 4 THEN '4 Credits'
    END AS Credits
 FROM students s
INNER JOIN enrolled_classes ec ON ec.student_id = s.student_id
ORDER BY s.student_id ASC
```

In this example, we take the class code and look at its first characters. Most class codes will be similar to *MATH 2433* or *ARTS 1123*. The first part of the class code indicates the class type, and the last number usually indicates the number of credits a course is worth. The first CASE statement we see takes the class_code and determines our class type (Math, Science, Chemistry, etc.). If there is no match, the ELSE statement will display the full class code (i.e., *ORG 1211*). The LIKE function does a fuzzy match on the value. Combined with the % symbol, we tell the case statement to do a hard match on the first characters in that order and accept any characters after, as denoted by the % symbol.

In the second CASE statement, we use the *RIGHT()* function to get the first character at the far right of the string. In this case, the last number of the class code. Using an equal qualifier, we determine the last number and then specify the number of credits as the value. Since our university example doesn't have course credits less than 1 or greater than 4, no ELSE statement exists. This is a good example of how the ELSE statement is optional.

The COALESCE statement emerges as a fundamental tool in SQL development, offering a concise solution for handling NULL values within queries. Let us delve into the versatility of the COALESCE statement, showcasing its ability to streamline data manipulation and enhance query results across diverse scenarios.

At its essence, the COALESCE statement is a powerful mechanism for substituting NULL values with alternate, non-NULL values. Whether you're dealing with data imports, joining tables, or performing calculations, the COALESCE statement provides a straightforward approach to managing NULLs effectively. By strategically incorporating COALESCE into your SQL queries, you can ensure data integrity, improve query readability, and mitigate potential errors arising from NULL handling.

Moreover, the COALESCE statement offers flexibility in handling multiple input values, allowing developers to prioritize values based on predefined preferences. This functionality is invaluable in scenarios where data quality or completeness varies across sources, enabling developers to prioritize fallback values or default options seamlessly. By harnessing the capabilities of the COALESCE statement, SQL developers can streamline data processing workflows and enhance the robustness of their query logic, ultimately contributing to more efficient and reliable data analysis.

The COALESCE statement in Snowflake returns the first non-NULL expression or NULL if all arguments are NULL. Let's look at an example.

Listing 5-2. Snowflake COALESCE query

```
SELECT column1, column2, column3, coalesce(column1, column2,
column3)
FROM (values
  (1,    2,    3  ),
  (null, 2,    3  ),
  (null, null, 3  ),
  (null, null, null),
  (1,    null, 3  ),
  (1,    null, null),
  (1,    2,    null)
) v;
```

COLUMN1	COLUMN2	COLUMN3	COALESCE(COLUMN1, COLUMN2, COLUMN3)
1	2	3	1
NULL	2	3	2
NULL	NULL	3	3
NULL	NULL	NULL	NULL
1	NULL	3	1
1	NULL	NULL	1
1	2	NULL	1

Figure 5-1. *COALESCE result set*

In the above example, the first row returns a value of 1 because column 1 is equal to 1. In the third row, the first two columns are NULL but the final column is equal to 3 so we return 3. In the fourth row, all three columns are NULL so the function returns NULL.

Handling Date and Time Data

Handling date and time data presents a critical aspect of data management and analysis, particularly in scenarios where temporal insights are pivotal. In this section, we explore best practices and techniques for effectively managing date and time data within Snowflake's SQL environment, empowering developers to extract meaningful insights and drive informed decision-making.

First and foremost, understanding the inherent complexities of date and time data is paramount. Snowflake offers a robust suite of functions and operators tailored to address various date and time-related tasks, from simple date arithmetic to sophisticated temporal calculations. By familiarizing themselves with these functions, developers can effortlessly manipulate date and time data, perform trend analysis, and derive actionable insights from temporal datasets.

Furthermore, ensuring data consistency and standardization is essential when working with date and time data. Snowflake's support for standardized date and time formats, alongside its comprehensive range of conversion functions, facilitates seamless data transformation and integration across diverse sources. Whether consolidating data from disparate systems or aligning data with organizational standards, Snowflake provides the tools necessary to streamline the process and maintain data integrity throughout the pipeline.

Finally, leveraging advanced features such as window functions and date-specific aggregation functions can enhance the depth and granularity of temporal analysis. Window functions enable developers to perform calculations over defined time intervals, facilitating trend analysis, moving averages, and other time-series operations. Similarly, date-specific aggregation functions such as DATE_TRUNC allow for summarizing data at various temporal granularities, empowering developers to extract insights at the desired level of detail. By harnessing these advanced capabilities, developers can unlock the full potential of date and time data within Snowflake, driving actionable insights and facilitating data-driven decision-making.

Snowflake supports over 20 date and time functions that you can use in your queries as well as commonly supported date and time parts. Because of various configuration options in Snowflake that can impact how dates and times are displayed, especially when working with timezones, it is recommended to perform your data and time manipulation using Laravel helper libraries and pass the data between your application and Snowflake. If you're doing this method, one of the most commonly used functions you might use in your SQL is the *TO_TIMESTAMP()* function. This lets you format both input and output data in Snowflake in a timestamp value that is easy to handle.

One thing to note is that the Snowflake API will pass data back to your application in EPOCH format. To convert this in Laravel, an example might look like Listing 5-3.

Listing 5-3. Laravel API handler with time values

```
$query = Http::withHeaders([
            'Content-Type' => 'application/json',
            'User-Agent' => 'myApplication/1.0',
            'X-Snowflake-Authorization-Token-Type' =>
            'KEYPAIR_JWT',
    ])->acceptJson()->withToken($jwt)->post
    ($snowflake_api_base_url.'/api/v2/statements', [
        'statement' => "SELECT CREATED_ON, ADDRESS,
        ZIP FROM customers;",
        'database' => $database,
        'warehouse' => $connection->warehouse,
        'schema' => $schema,
```

```
        'role' => $connection->role,
        'parameters' => [
            'query_tag' => 'black-diamond',
        ],
    ]);
$epoch = $query['data'][0][0];
$dt = new DateTime("@$epoch");
echo $dt->format('Y-m-d H:i:s');
```

The above code will pull the first record and the first column, the CREATED_ON column, and assign the epoch value to a variable. It then uses the DateTime library to set it as an epoch datetime value, and then we format it to a human-readable format.

Dynamic SQL and Stored Procedures

Dynamic SQL represents a versatile approach to SQL query construction, allowing developers to generate and execute SQL statements dynamically at runtime. This capability is particularly valuable in scenarios where the structure or content of queries may vary based on user inputs, data conditions, or application logic. In this section, we delve into the intricacies of dynamic SQL within the context of Snowflake, exploring its benefits, challenges, and best practices for implementation.

One of the key advantages of dynamic SQL is its flexibility in adapting to changing requirements and dynamic data environments. By generating SQL statements dynamically, developers can construct queries tailored to specific use cases, conditions, or user preferences. This flexibility extends to scenarios such as ad-hoc reporting, data-driven application logic, and dynamic filtering, where the ability to construct SQL statements on the fly enhances the agility and responsiveness of the system. However, dynamic

SQL also introduces considerations related to security, performance, and maintainability, requiring careful planning and adherence to best practices to mitigate potential risks and ensure optimal query execution.

Stored procedures serve as a powerful tool for encapsulating SQL logic within Snowflake, enabling developers to execute complex operations, transactions, and business logic on the server side. In essence, stored procedures are precompiled SQL code blocks stored in the database and executed on demand. In this section, we explore the benefits and functionalities of stored procedures within Snowflake, highlighting their role in enhancing performance, security, and maintainability in data-driven applications.

One of the primary advantages of stored procedures is their ability to streamline database operations by centralizing and standardizing SQL logic. By encapsulating commonly used queries, data transformations, and business rules within stored procedures, developers can promote code reuse, minimize redundancy, and improve overall code maintainability. Moreover, stored procedures facilitate modular development practices, allowing developers to break down complex tasks into smaller, manageable units of code. This modular approach not only enhances code organization but also simplifies debugging, testing, and version control, leading to more robust and scalable database applications.

Let's assume we have a list of stored procedures we want to call all at once in our DATAVAULT. We can send a dynamic query to Snowflake to get a callable list of stored procedures like in Listing 5-4.

Listing 5-4. Snowflake stored procedure dictionary

```
SELECT 'CALL ' || PROCEDURE_CATALOG || '.' || PROCEDURE_SCHEMA
|| '.' || PROCEDURE_NAME || '();' cmd
FROM datavault.information_schema.procedures
WHERE PROCEDURE_CATALOG = 'DATAVAULT' AND PROCEDURE_SCHEMA
= 'SOURCE';
```

The above example might output a list of stored procedures in the format *CALL SPROC_NAME();*. This list might look something like Listing 5-5.

Listing 5-5. Laravel REST API handler for stored procedures

```
$sprocs = $query['data'];
foreach ($sprocs AS $sproc)
{
$query2 = Http::withHeaders([
            'Content-Type' => 'application/json',
            'User-Agent' => 'myApplication/1.0',
            'X-Snowflake-Authorization-Token-Type' =>
            'KEYPAIR_JWT',
        ])->acceptJson()->withToken($jwt)->post
        ($snowflake_api_base_url.'/api/v2/statements', [
            'statement' => $sproc[0],
            'database' => $database,
            'warehouse' => $connection->warehouse,
            'schema' => $schema,
            'role' => $connection->role,
            'parameters' => [
                'query_tag' => 'black-diamond',
            ],
        ]);
        wait 5;
}
```

The above code will take the list of stored procedures and call each one. We put in a wait of 5 seconds at the end of the foreach loop to prevent too many queries from queuing up at the same time and relieve some of the load from our Snowflake Warehouse.

User-Defined Functions (UDFs)

User-defined functions (UDFs) play a pivotal role in extending the functionality of SQL queries within Snowflake, empowering developers to implement custom logic and computations tailored to specific requirements. In essence, UDFs allow developers to encapsulate complex algorithms or business logic into reusable code snippets, which can then be seamlessly integrated into SQL queries. In this section, we delve into the versatility and utility of UDFs within Snowflake, exploring their applications across various use cases and scenarios.

One of the key benefits of UDFs is their ability to enhance query expressiveness and readability by abstracting complex operations into concise and intuitive function calls. Whether performing data transformations, calculations, or string manipulations, UDFs provide a streamlined approach to implementing custom logic within SQL queries. By encapsulating complex operations within reusable functions, developers can promote code reuse, improve code maintainability, and reduce the risk of errors or inconsistencies across queries.

Furthermore, UDFs enable developers to extend the native capabilities of Snowflake's SQL engine, facilitating the implementation of specialized algorithms or computations that are not natively supported by built-in SQL functions. Whether implementing custom statistical functions, geospatial calculations, or domain-specific logic, UDFs empower developers to address unique requirements and extract valuable insights from data. Additionally, UDFs can be leveraged to encapsulate common data processing tasks, such as data cleansing, validation, or enrichment, streamlining data preparation workflows and enhancing the efficiency of data processing pipelines.

Snowflake allows you to create UDFs using Java, JavaScript, Python, and SQL. If using JavaScript or SQL, you do not have to define the HANDLER type in the creation of your function as these are automatically identified by Snowflake. In data science applications, a UDF might be created to scrub data and return it to a stored procedure to then be processed in Scala or Python via Snowpark.

CHAPTER 6

Data Security and Access Control

In the digital age, data security and access control stand as paramount concerns for organizations across industries, as the proliferation of data brings with it an increased risk of unauthorized access, breaches, and data loss. This chapter delves into the foundational principles and best practices of data security and access control within Snowflake, empowering organizations to safeguard their data assets and mitigate security risks effectively.

At the heart of data security lies the principle of confidentiality, ensuring that sensitive information remains accessible only to authorized users. Snowflake offers a comprehensive suite of security features to protect data at rest and in transit, including encryption, tokenization, and secure data-sharing capabilities. Additionally, Snowflake's robust authentication and authorization mechanisms enable organizations to control access to data resources based on user roles, permissions, and privileges, ensuring that only authorized users can view, modify, or delete data. By implementing these security measures, organizations can maintain the confidentiality of their data assets and protect against unauthorized access or data breaches.

© Ronald Steelman 2024
R. Steelman, *Mastering the Snowflake SQL API with Laravel 10*, Apress Pocket Guides,
https://doi.org/10.1007/979-8-8688-0382-6_6

Authentication and Authorization

Snowflake's authentication and authorization mechanisms form the cornerstone of its robust security architecture, ensuring the confidentiality, integrity, and availability of data within the platform. Authentication in Snowflake revolves around user authentication and identity verification, typically through username/password credentials or federated authentication methods such as SAML or OAuth. This ensures that only authorized users can access Snowflake resources, minimizing the risk of unauthorized access and data breaches. Additionally, Snowflake supports multi-factor authentication (MFA), adding an extra layer of security by requiring users to provide multiple forms of authentication before accessing their accounts.

Authorization in Snowflake governs access control and permissions management, dictating what actions users and roles can perform on specific resources within the platform. Snowflake employs a role-based access control (RBAC) model, where permissions are assigned to roles, and users are granted access to resources by inheriting roles. This hierarchical approach allows for granular control over access rights, ensuring that users have the necessary privileges to perform their tasks while preventing unauthorized access to sensitive data or operations. Moreover, Snowflake offers fine-grained access control capabilities, allowing administrators to define custom roles and permissions tailored to the unique requirements of their organization.

To further enhance security, Snowflake provides comprehensive auditing and monitoring features, enabling administrators to track user activity, access attempts, and data modifications in real time. This audit trail provides visibility into who accessed what data and when, facilitating compliance with regulatory requirements and internal security policies. Additionally, Snowflake integrates with external identity providers and security information and event management (SIEM) solutions, allowing organizations to centralize authentication and authorization management and streamline security operations. Overall, Snowflake's robust authentication and authorization mechanisms ensure that data remains protected and accessible only to authorized users, maintaining the integrity and trustworthiness of the platform.

One example of Snowflake authentication is through the use of username and password credentials. Users can authenticate themselves by providing their username and password when accessing Snowflake's services through various client applications or interfaces. Upon successful authentication, Snowflake verifies the provided credentials against its authentication system to validate the user's identity. This process ensures that only users with valid credentials can access Snowflake resources, maintaining the security and integrity of the platform.

Additionally, Snowflake supports federated authentication methods such as Security Assertion Markup Language (SAML) and OAuth, allowing organizations to integrate their existing identity providers (IdPs) with Snowflake for single sign-on (SSO) capabilities. With federated authentication, users can authenticate using their existing corporate credentials, eliminating the need for separate Snowflake-specific credentials and streamlining the authentication process. This integration enhances security by centralizing identity management and enforcing organizational authentication policies across all applications and services, including Snowflake.

An example of Snowflake authorization is the implementation of role-based access control (RBAC) to manage user permissions and access privileges within the platform. In this scenario, Snowflake administrators define roles that encapsulate specific sets of permissions corresponding to different levels of access to data and resources. For instance, roles may be created for data analysts, data engineers, and administrators, each with varying degrees of access rights tailored to their respective responsibilities.

Once roles are defined, users are assigned to these roles based on their job functions or organizational hierarchy. Users inherit the permissions associated with the roles to which they are assigned, dictating what actions they can perform within Snowflake. For example, a data analyst role might have read-only access to certain databases or tables, while a data engineer role might have permissions to create and modify objects within the database. By leveraging role-based authorization, Snowflake ensures that users have appropriate access to data resources while maintaining security and compliance with organizational policies and regulations.

Role-Based Access Control (RBAC)

Role-based access control (RBAC) stands as a foundational principle in Snowflake's security architecture, offering a robust framework for managing user permissions and access privileges within the platform. In this section, we explore the principles and practices of RBAC within Snowflake, highlighting its significance in enforcing security policies, promoting data governance, and facilitating granular access control.

At its core, RBAC revolves around the concept of roles, which encapsulate specific sets of permissions corresponding to different user responsibilities or job functions. Snowflake administrators define roles based on the principle of least privilege, assigning only the necessary permissions required for users to perform their tasks effectively. This granular approach ensures that users have access to precisely the resources they need while minimizing the risk of unauthorized access or data breaches.

Furthermore, RBAC in Snowflake enables administrators to manage access control dynamically, allowing for flexible assignment and modification of roles based on evolving business requirements. Whether provisioning new users, updating permissions, or revoking access, administrators can adapt access controls to align with organizational changes, ensuring that security policies remain relevant and effective over time. By leveraging RBAC, organizations can establish a robust security posture within Snowflake, mitigating risks and safeguarding their data assets against unauthorized access or misuse.

Consider a scenario where a large e-commerce company utilizes Snowflake for managing its data infrastructure. Within this organization, different teams have varying responsibilities and data access requirements. The IT operations team is responsible for managing the underlying infrastructure and system configurations, while the data engineering team oversees data pipelines, transformations, and warehouse management. Meanwhile, the analytics team focuses on deriving insights from the data to support business decision-making.

In Snowflake, administrators create distinct roles tailored to each team's responsibilities. For instance, they establish an "IT Operations" role with permissions to manage virtual warehouses, monitor system health, and perform system-level configurations. The "Data Engineering" role is granted permissions to create and manage databases, tables, and views, as well as to execute ETL processes and data loading tasks. Lastly, the "Analytics" role is assigned read-only access to specific datasets and analytical views, enabling team members to run queries and generate reports without modifying the underlying data.

By implementing role-based access control in Snowflake, the e-commerce company ensures that each team has access to the resources and functionalities required to fulfill their respective duties while adhering to the principle of least privilege. Additionally, as organizational needs evolve, administrators can easily modify role assignments and permissions to accommodate changes in team structures or data access requirements, maintaining a secure and compliant data environment within Snowflake.

Data Masking and Row-Level Security

Snowflake's data masking policies provide a robust mechanism for protecting sensitive data and preserving confidentiality within the platform. With data privacy regulations becoming increasingly stringent, organizations must ensure that sensitive information such as personally identifiable information (PII) and financial data remains secure, even during data processing and analytics operations. Snowflake's data masking policies offer a comprehensive solution to this challenge by enabling organizations to define and enforce masking rules that obfuscate sensitive data while preserving its utility for analysis and reporting.

Using Snowflake's data masking policies, administrators can implement a variety of masking techniques to anonymize or redact sensitive information based on predefined rules. For example, organizations may choose to apply format-preserving encryption to sensitive fields, ensuring that the masked data retains its original format and structure while rendering it unreadable to unauthorized users. Alternatively, masking policies can be configured to replace sensitive values with pseudonymized or tokenized representations, preserving the integrity of the data for analytical purposes while preventing unauthorized access to sensitive information.

Furthermore, Snowflake's data masking policies support dynamic masking based on user roles or contextual attributes, allowing organizations to tailor masking behavior to specific use cases or access scenarios. For instance, administrators can define different masking policies for internal users, external partners, or regulatory compliance purposes, ensuring that sensitive data is protected consistently across diverse data consumption scenarios. By leveraging Snowflake's data masking capabilities, organizations can bolster their data security posture, comply with regulatory requirements, and mitigate the risk of data breaches or privacy violations, all while enabling secure and compliant data analytics within the platform.

Listing 6-1. Snowflake masking policy dictionary

```
CREATE OR REPLACE MASKING POLICY ssn_mask AS (val string)
RETURNS string ->
    CASE
```

```
WHEN CURRENT_ROLE() IN ('HR') THEN val
  ELSE '*** - *** - ****'
END;
```

```
ALTER TABLE IF EXISTS employee_info MODIFY COLUMN ssn SET
MASKING POLICY ssn_mask;
```

The above code creates a data mask to hide social security numbers from everyone except those in the HR role. We then alter the employee table to apply the mask to the SSN column. Now, anytime a user not in the HR role queries that column, they will see a masked value. This allows for only HR users to view social security numbers for employees while protecting those employees from other users.

Security Best Practices in Snowflake

Snowflake offers a plethora of security features and functionalities to help organizations safeguard their data assets and ensure compliance with regulatory requirements. To leverage these capabilities effectively, it's essential to adhere to security best practices tailored to Snowflake's unique architecture and capabilities.

First and foremost, organizations should adopt a robust authentication and access control strategy. This includes implementing multi-factor authentication (MFA) to add an extra layer of security for user authentication. Additionally, organizations should leverage role-based access control (RBAC) to define granular permissions and access levels for users and roles. By following the principle of least privilege, organizations can ensure that users only have access to the data and resources necessary to perform their job functions.

Encryption is another critical aspect of Snowflake security best practices. Organizations should encrypt data both at rest and in transit using Snowflake's native encryption capabilities. This includes encrypting data stored in Snowflake's cloud storage and encrypting data transmitted between Snowflake and client applications using SSL/TLS encryption. By encrypting data end-to-end, organizations can protect sensitive information from unauthorized access and mitigate the risk of data breaches.

Furthermore, organizations should implement robust monitoring and auditing mechanisms to track user activity and detect suspicious behavior. Snowflake provides comprehensive auditing capabilities that enable organizations to monitor user actions, access attempts, and data modifications in real time. By regularly reviewing audit logs and analyzing security events, organizations can identify potential security threats and take proactive measures to mitigate risks.

Data masking and anonymization are essential security best practices for protecting sensitive data within Snowflake. Organizations should implement data masking policies to obfuscate sensitive information such as personally identifiable information (PII) and financial data. This helps prevent unauthorized access to sensitive data while preserving its utility for analytics and reporting purposes. Additionally, organizations should leverage Snowflake's data tokenization capabilities to tokenize sensitive data fields, further enhancing data security and privacy.

In summary, Snowflake security best practices encompass a range of measures, including robust authentication and access control, encryption, monitoring and auditing, and data masking. By following these best practices, organizations can strengthen their data security posture, comply with regulatory requirements, and mitigate the risk of data breaches or privacy violations in Snowflake.

Performance Tuning and Optimization

Optimizing performance in Snowflake is crucial for ensuring that data processing and analytics operations are executed efficiently and deliver timely insights to users. As organizations accumulate vast amounts of data, optimizing query performance becomes paramount to maintain responsiveness and meet business objectives. In this section, we delve into the fundamentals of performance tuning and optimization within Snowflake, exploring techniques and best practices to enhance query execution speed, minimize resource utilization, and maximize overall system efficiency.

At the core of Snowflake performance tuning lies the understanding of Snowflake's unique architecture and query execution model. Snowflake's architecture, built on a multi-cluster, shared-storage model, offers unparalleled scalability and concurrency for data processing. However, optimizing performance requires a nuanced approach, considering factors such as data distribution, query complexity, and resource allocation. By gaining insights into Snowflake's query processing engine, query optimization techniques, and execution plans, organizations can identify performance bottlenecks and implement targeted optimizations to improve query performance.

Moreover, performance tuning in Snowflake encompasses a range of strategies, including optimizing SQL queries, tuning virtual warehouses, and leveraging caching and materialized views. By optimizing SQL queries,

R. Steelman, *Mastering the Snowflake SQL API with Laravel 10*, Apress Pocket Guides, https://doi.org/10.1007/979-8-8688-0382-6_7

organizations can improve query efficiency by minimizing data scans, reducing computational overhead, and optimizing join operations. Tuning virtual warehouses involves configuring warehouse sizes, auto-scaling policies, and concurrency settings to ensure optimal resource allocation and performance for different workloads. Additionally, caching and materialized views can be leveraged to store and precompute query results, reducing query processing time and enhancing overall system performance. Through a comprehensive approach to performance tuning and optimization, organizations can unlock the full potential of Snowflake's data warehousing platform, enabling faster and more efficient data analytics and decision-making processes.

Understanding Query Execution

Understanding Snowflake query execution is essential for optimizing performance and maximizing the efficiency of data processing operations within the platform. Snowflake's query execution model is based on a distributed, multi-cluster architecture, designed to scale horizontally and handle concurrent user workloads seamlessly. In this section, we explore the key components and stages of Snowflake query execution, shedding light on the intricacies of how queries are processed and executed within the platform.

At a high level, Snowflake query execution comprises several stages, including parsing, optimization, compilation, execution, and result retrieval. When a query is submitted to Snowflake, it undergoes a parsing phase where the SQL statement is analyzed and broken down into a parse tree representation. This parse tree is then optimized by Snowflake's query optimizer, which evaluates various query execution strategies, access paths, and join orders to generate an optimal query plan. Once optimized, the query plan is compiled into executable code and distributed across multiple compute nodes within Snowflake's virtual warehouses.

During execution, each compute node independently processes a portion of the query plan, executing tasks such as scanning data from storage, performing computations, and aggregating results. Snowflake's dynamic optimization capabilities allow it to adapt to changing workload conditions in real time, automatically adjusting resource allocation and query execution strategies to optimize performance. Finally, the results from each compute node are aggregated and merged to produce the final query output, which is then returned to the user.

By understanding the intricacies of Snowflake query execution, organizations can identify opportunities for optimization and fine-tuning to improve query performance and resource utilization. Techniques such as query profiling, explain plans, and performance monitoring can provide valuable insights into query execution behavior, helping organizations identify bottlenecks, optimize resource allocation, and streamline data processing workflows. With a deeper understanding of Snowflake query execution, organizations can unlock the full potential of the platform for fast, efficient, and scalable data analytics and decision-making.

Consider a scenario where a data analyst in a retail company submits a SQL query to Snowflake to analyze sales data for a specific product category. Upon receiving the query, Snowflake's query processing engine begins the execution process. First, the SQL query undergoes parsing, where it is analyzed and broken down into a parse tree representation to identify the query's structure and components. Next, the query optimizer evaluates various query execution strategies and optimization techniques to generate an optimal query plan based on factors such as data distribution, indexing, and join order.

Once optimized, the query plan is compiled into executable code and distributed across multiple compute nodes within Snowflake's virtual warehouses. Each compute node independently processes a portion of the query plan, scanning relevant data from Snowflake's shared-storage architecture, and performing aggregations, and computations as necessary. Snowflake's dynamic optimization capabilities ensure that resources are allocated efficiently, and query execution adapts to changing workload conditions in real time. Finally, the results from each compute node are aggregated and merged to produce the final query output, which is then returned to the data analyst for further analysis and decision-making. Through this example, we can see how Snowflake's distributed query execution model enables fast, scalable, and efficient data processing for complex analytical queries.

Query Profiling and Monitoring

Snowflake query profiling and monitoring play pivotal roles in maintaining optimal performance and identifying opportunities for optimization within the platform. Query profiling involves analyzing the execution characteristics and resource utilization of individual SQL queries to gain insights into their performance. Meanwhile, query monitoring provides real-time visibility into query execution, allowing organizations to track query progress, identify bottlenecks, and troubleshoot performance issues as they arise.

One of the key features of Snowflake query profiling is the ability to generate explain plans, which provide a detailed breakdown of how a query is executed within Snowflake's distributed architecture. Explain plans reveal crucial information such as data distribution, join order, access paths, and estimated query costs, enabling organizations to understand the underlying execution strategy and identify potential areas for optimization. By analyzing explain plans, organizations can gain insights into query performance characteristics, such as data skew, partition pruning, and resource contention, allowing them to fine-tune queries and optimize resource utilization.

Additionally, Snowflake provides comprehensive performance monitoring capabilities that enable organizations to track query execution metrics in real time. Through Snowflake's web interface or third-party monitoring tools, organizations can monitor query execution progress, resource consumption, and concurrency levels, gaining visibility into the overall health and performance of their data processing workloads. By monitoring query performance metrics over time, organizations can identify trends, detect anomalies, and proactively address performance issues before they impact critical business operations.

Furthermore, Snowflake offers advanced diagnostic tools and performance monitoring features, such as query history and query execution statistics, which enable organizations to analyze historical query performance and identify recurring patterns or trends. By leveraging these tools, organizations can gain deeper insights into query behavior, identify long-running or resource-intensive queries, and optimize query performance accordingly. Overall, Snowflake query profiling and monitoring provide organizations with the visibility and insights needed to optimize query performance, enhance resource utilization, and maximize the efficiency of their data processing workflows.

In a real-world scenario, let's consider a multinational e-commerce company that utilizes Snowflake for its data analytics and reporting needs. One of their critical business processes involves analyzing customer behavior to optimize marketing campaigns and drive sales. The company regularly runs complex SQL queries to segment customers based on demographics, purchase history, and browsing behavior, among other factors.

To ensure optimal query performance and resource utilization, the company leverages Snowflake's query profiling and monitoring capabilities. Before executing a new query, analysts use Snowflake's explain plan feature to generate a detailed breakdown of the query execution strategy. For instance, they may examine how Snowflake plans to distribute the query workload across compute clusters and identify any potential inefficiencies or bottlenecks in the execution plan.

As queries are executed, the company monitors query performance metrics in real time using Snowflake's monitoring tools. They track key metrics such as query execution time, resource consumption, and concurrency levels to ensure that queries are running efficiently and within expected performance thresholds. If a query starts to exhibit signs of performance degradation or resource contention, administrators receive alerts, allowing them to investigate the issue promptly and take corrective action, such as adjusting warehouse sizes or optimizing query logic.

By leveraging Snowflake's query profiling and monitoring capabilities, the e-commerce company can optimize query performance, minimize resource usage, and ensure timely insights for informed decision-making. This proactive approach to query optimization enables the company to maintain a competitive edge in the dynamic e-commerce landscape by delivering targeted marketing campaigns, personalized recommendations, and superior customer experiences based on real-time data analysis.

Query Optimization Techniques

Snowflake offers a range of query optimization techniques to enhance performance and efficiency in data processing operations. These techniques leverage Snowflake's distributed architecture and dynamic optimization capabilities to optimize query execution plans and minimize resource consumption. Let's explore some key optimization techniques along with examples.

Let's first look at query rewriting strategies. Query rewriting involves restructuring SQL queries to improve performance by minimizing data scans and reducing computational overhead. For example, consider a query that retrieves sales data for a specific product category. By restructuring the query to leverage predicate pushdown and filter out irrelevant data early in the query execution process, Snowflake can optimize performance by reducing the amount of data scanned and processed.

The next thing we should look at when optimizing our queries are any joins we have and how to optimize joins. Snowflake provides various optimization techniques for optimizing join operations, such as selecting appropriate join algorithms, optimizing join order, and leveraging join hints. For instance, suppose a query involves joining large fact tables with dimension tables. Snowflake's query optimizer can automatically select the optimal join algorithm (e.g., hash join or merge join) based on data distribution statistics and join cardinality estimates to minimize query execution time and resource usage.

After we have performed any query modifications and join optimizations, we should then look at partition pruning. Partition pruning is a technique used to optimize queries by eliminating unnecessary partitions from data scans based on predicate filters. For example, suppose a query retrieves sales data for a specific date range. Snowflake's query optimizer can leverage partition pruning to scan only the relevant partitions containing data within the specified date range, reducing the amount of data scanned and improving query performance significantly.

Outside of reviewing and updating the query in question, we can also focus on optimizing warehouse configurations. Snowflake offers various configuration options for optimizing virtual warehouses, such as adjusting warehouse sizes, concurrency settings, and auto-scaling policies. For example, suppose a query workload experiences fluctuating demand throughout the day. By configuring virtual warehouses with auto-scaling policies, Snowflake can dynamically adjust warehouse sizes based on workload requirements, ensuring optimal resource allocation and query performance during peak usage periods. Remember that larger warehouses allow you to crunch through data faster helping to eliminate spilling to disk which can be much slower in an instance where we can't reduce the partitions any further, while scaling allows a warehouse to run multiple queries in parallel while cutting down on queuing.

If your data updates only infrequently, a great mechanism is to leverage materialized views and caching. Snowflake supports materialized views and caching mechanisms to improve query performance by precomputing and caching query results. For example, consider a complex analytical query that aggregates sales data across multiple dimensions.

By creating a materialized view that precomputes the aggregated results, Snowflake can accelerate query execution by retrieving cached results from the materialized view instead of recalculating the aggregation on-the-fly.

By leveraging these query optimization techniques, organizations can enhance query performance, minimize resource utilization, and maximize the efficiency of their data processing workflows within Snowflake. These optimizations enable organizations to deliver faster insights, improve decision-making processes, and derive greater value from their data assets.

Snowflake Resource Management

Snowflake offers comprehensive resource management capabilities to ensure efficient allocation and utilization of computing resources within the platform. Resource management in Snowflake encompasses various features and functionalities, including virtual warehouses, resource monitors, and workload management policies. These capabilities enable organizations to optimize performance, control costs, and manage concurrency effectively.

At the core of Snowflake's resource management is the concept of virtual warehouses, which are compute clusters that execute SQL queries and data processing tasks. Organizations can create multiple virtual warehouses with different configurations, such as size, scaling policies, and concurrency limits, to cater to diverse workload requirements. For example, a company may create separate virtual warehouses for ad hoc analytics, batch processing, and data loading tasks, each with its own resource allocation settings to prioritize and optimize performance for specific workloads.

Additionally, Snowflake offers resource monitors, which provide real-time visibility into resource usage and performance metrics for virtual warehouses. Resource monitors allow organizations to track key metrics such as CPU utilization, storage usage, and query concurrency levels, enabling them to monitor workload performance, identify bottlenecks, and troubleshoot performance issues proactively. For example, if a virtual warehouse is experiencing high CPU usage or query concurrency, administrators can adjust warehouse sizes or concurrency limits to optimize resource utilization and ensure smooth query execution.

Furthermore, Snowflake's workload management capabilities enable organizations to define and enforce policies for prioritizing and managing query execution within virtual warehouses. Workload management policies allow organizations to allocate resources based on business priorities, workload characteristics, and user roles. For instance, administrators can configure workload management policies to prioritize critical business queries over less time-sensitive workloads, ensuring that resources are allocated appropriately to meet SLAs and business objectives. By leveraging Snowflake's resource management capabilities, organizations can optimize performance, control costs, and deliver consistent and reliable query processing across diverse workloads within the platform.

It is always recommended to set up resource monitors in Snowflake to alert you on specific thresholds on each warehouse letting you know when those thresholds are met or exceeded. You can further leverage resource monitors to prevent errant queries from hanging and consuming credits by putting a monthly throttle on how many credits a warehouse can consume each month. If a greater credit consumption occurs and this is expected, you can increase that limit.

Warehouse Caching

Snowflake's warehouse caching feature is a powerful mechanism for improving query performance and reducing data processing latency by caching query results in memory. When enabled, Snowflake automatically caches frequently accessed data blocks and query results within the virtual warehouse's cache, allowing subsequent queries to retrieve data from the cache rather than performing disk I/O operations. This results in faster query execution times and improved responsiveness for analytical workloads.

For example, consider a retail company that frequently runs ad hoc queries to analyze sales data across different regions and product categories. With warehouse caching enabled, Snowflake caches commonly accessed data blocks and query results in the virtual warehouse's cache. As a result, when analysts execute similar queries, Snowflake can retrieve data directly from the cache, eliminating the need to access data from disk storage. This leads to significant performance improvements and faster query response times, enabling analysts to derive insights more quickly and make timely business decisions.

Furthermore, warehouse caching in Snowflake is dynamic and adaptive, meaning that the cache is continuously updated and optimized based on query patterns, data access frequencies, and available memory resources. For instance, if a particular query result is frequently accessed, Snowflake may prioritize caching that data in memory to expedite subsequent query executions. Similarly, if memory resources become constrained or query patterns change, Snowflake may evict less frequently accessed data from the cache to make room for more relevant data, ensuring optimal cache utilization and performance for varying workloads.

Overall, Snowflake's warehouse caching feature provides organizations with a powerful tool for improving query performance, reducing latency, and enhancing the overall efficiency of data processing operations within the platform. By leveraging warehouse caching, organizations can accelerate analytical queries, streamline data analysis workflows, and derive insights more quickly from their data assets, ultimately driving better decision-making and business outcomes.

CHAPTER 8

Data Warehousing Best Practices

This chapter serves as a foundational guide for organizations seeking to optimize their data warehousing strategies within Snowflake. In the modern data landscape, effective data warehousing is essential for unlocking the full potential of data assets, enabling informed decision-making, and driving business growth. This chapter delves into proven best practices, methodologies, and techniques for designing, implementing, and managing data warehouses within Snowflake to maximize performance, scalability, and efficiency.

At its core, effective data warehousing requires a holistic approach that encompasses various aspects, including data modeling, schema design, data loading strategies, and query optimization. By adopting best practices in these areas, organizations can design data warehouses that are well-structured, efficient, and capable of meeting evolving business requirements. For example, organizations may adopt dimensional modeling techniques to design star schemas or snowflake schemas that optimize query performance and facilitate intuitive data analysis and reporting.

Furthermore, this chapter explores strategies for data governance, security, and compliance within Snowflake data warehouses. Data governance is crucial for ensuring data quality, consistency, and integrity across the organization, while security and compliance measures help

© Ronald Steelman 2024
R. Steelman, *Mastering the Snowflake SQL API with Laravel 10*, Apress Pocket Guides,
https://doi.org/10.1007/979-8-8688-0382-6_8

protect sensitive data and ensure regulatory adherence. By implementing best practices for data governance, organizations can establish standardized processes for data management, lineage tracking, and metadata management, fostering a culture of data-driven decision-making and accountability. Additionally, robust security measures, such as encryption, access controls, and auditing, safeguard data assets from unauthorized access, ensuring confidentiality and compliance with regulatory requirements. Through this comprehensive approach to data warehousing best practices, organizations can build scalable, reliable, and secure data warehouses within Snowflake that serve as a foundation for driving business success and innovation.

Data Modeling in Snowflake

Data modeling in Snowflake involves designing logical and physical schemas that organize and structure data within the platform to facilitate efficient querying, analysis, and reporting. This section on data modeling best practices explores methodologies and techniques for designing effective data models within Snowflake to meet business requirements, optimize query performance, and ensure data consistency and integrity.

One of the key best practices in data modeling within Snowflake is adopting dimensional modeling techniques, such as star schemas or snowflake schemas, for organizing data in data warehouses. Dimensional modeling simplifies data analysis by organizing data into fact tables (containing measures) and dimension tables (containing descriptive attributes), enabling intuitive querying and reporting. By leveraging dimensional modeling, organizations can optimize query performance, reduce data redundancy, and improve data accessibility for end-users.

Additionally, there are strategies for designing flexible and scalable data models that can accommodate evolving business requirements and data sources. Snowflake's support for semi-structured data formats such as JSON and VARIANT data types enables organizations to store and query diverse data types within the same data warehouse. Best practices for incorporating semi-structured data into data models involve leveraging nested data structures, using VARIANT columns to store complex data types, and optimizing queries to handle semi-structured data efficiently.

Furthermore, we can look at optimizing data modeling for Snowflake's distributed architecture and query processing capabilities. Snowflake's virtual warehouses allow organizations to scale compute resources dynamically to handle varying workload demands. Best practices for data modeling in Snowflake involve designing schemas that distribute data evenly across compute nodes, minimizing data skew, and optimizing data locality for efficient query execution. Additionally, organizations can leverage Snowflake's clustering keys to physically organize data within tables based on common query patterns, further improving query performance and resource utilization. Through these best practices, organizations can design scalable, efficient, and flexible data models within Snowflake that empower users to derive actionable insights and drive business success.

Snowflake Clustering Keys

Snowflake clustering keys are a powerful feature for optimizing query performance by physically organizing data within tables based on common query patterns. Clustering keys determine the order in which data is stored on disk, allowing Snowflake to group related data together and minimize the need for disk I/O operations during query execution. This section explores best practices and examples for leveraging clustering keys effectively within Snowflake to improve query performance and resource utilization.

One example of leveraging clustering keys is in a sales data warehouse where queries frequently filter data based on the date of the sale. By defining a clustering key on the sales date column, Snowflake organizes data within the table based on the date of the sale, physically grouping together records with similar dates. As a result, queries that filter data by sales date benefit from improved query performance, as Snowflake can quickly locate and access relevant data blocks on disk without scanning unnecessary data.

Furthermore, clustering keys can be used to optimize queries that involve joins between multiple tables. For example, consider a data warehouse that stores sales transactions in one table and customer information in another table. By defining clustering keys on the join columns (e.g., customer ID) in both tables, Snowflake can physically organize data based on customer IDs, aligning related records from both tables on disk. As a result, join operations between the tables are more efficient, as Snowflake can minimize data movement and perform join operations locally within each compute node.

Additionally, clustering keys can be used to optimize queries that involve range-based or inequality predicates. For instance, suppose a query filters sales data based on a range of sales amounts or a specific region. By defining a clustering key on the relevant column (e.g., sales amount or region), Snowflake can organize data within the table based on the values of that column, improving query performance for range-based queries. Snowflake's automatic clustering feature can also be leveraged to dynamically maintain clustering keys based on data access patterns and query workload, ensuring optimal data organization and query performance over time.

Overall, Snowflake clustering keys are a valuable tool for optimizing query performance and resource utilization within data warehouses. By strategically defining clustering keys based on common query patterns and access patterns, organizations can significantly improve query performance, reduce latency, and enhance the overall efficiency of their data processing workflows within Snowflake.

Partitioning Data for Efficiency

Partitioning data for efficiency is a crucial aspect of optimizing data storage and query performance within Snowflake. By partitioning data based on specific criteria, organizations can improve query performance, reduce data scanning, and enhance overall system efficiency. This section explores best practices and examples for partitioning data within Snowflake to maximize efficiency and scalability.

One common approach to partitioning data in Snowflake is time-based partitioning, where data is partitioned based on temporal attributes such as date or timestamp. For example, consider a retail company that stores historical sales data in a data warehouse. By partitioning the sales data table based on the sales date, Snowflake can organize data into separate partitions for each time period (e.g., day, week, or month). This allows Snowflake to prune unnecessary partitions during query execution, significantly reducing data scanning and improving query performance for time-based queries.

Another example of partitioning data for efficiency is geographical partitioning, where data is partitioned based on geographic attributes such as region or country. For instance, a global e-commerce company may partition customer data based on the customer's country of residence. By partitioning data geographically, Snowflake can optimize queries that filter or aggregate data based on geographic criteria, minimizing data movement and improving query performance for location-based analyses.

Furthermore, organizations can leverage custom partitioning strategies tailored to their specific business requirements and query patterns. For example, a financial institution may partition transaction data based on transaction type or account ID to optimize queries related to specific types of transactions or individual accounts. By defining custom partitioning schemes, organizations can align data storage and query execution with their business logic and access patterns, maximizing efficiency and performance within Snowflake.

Overall, partitioning data for efficiency is a powerful technique for optimizing query performance and resource utilization within Snowflake. By partitioning data based on relevant criteria such as time, geography, or custom attributes, organizations can streamline data access, reduce data scanning, and improve overall system efficiency, enabling faster and more scalable data processing workflows within the platform.

Data Compression Strategies

Data compression strategies play a significant role in optimizing storage utilization and query performance within Snowflake. By compressing data before storing it in the platform, organizations can reduce storage costs, minimize disk space usage, and improve query performance by reducing data transfer and I/O operations. This section explores various data compression strategies available in Snowflake, along with examples of how they can be applied to optimize data storage and query performance.

One common data compression strategy in Snowflake is columnar compression, where data within individual columns is compressed using columnar compression algorithms such as run-length encoding (RLE) or dictionary encoding. For example, consider a sales data table with multiple columns representing attributes such as product ID, customer ID, and sales amount. By compressing each column independently using columnar compression techniques, Snowflake can reduce the storage footprint of the table and improve query performance by minimizing disk I/O operations during query execution.

Another example of data compression in Snowflake is block-level compression, where data blocks are compressed at the block level before being stored on disk. Snowflake automatically applies block-level compression to data blocks within storage, using compression algorithms such as LZ4 or Zstandard to compress data efficiently. For instance, when ingesting large volumes of semi-structured data such as JSON or

AVRO files into Snowflake, block-level compression helps reduce storage overhead and improve data transfer speeds, enabling faster data loading and query performance.

Furthermore, Snowflake supports automatic data compression, where the platform automatically applies compression to data based on its characteristics and usage patterns. For example, Snowflake may identify columns with high redundancy or low cardinality and apply compression algorithms such as dictionary encoding to optimize storage utilization. Additionally, Snowflake's automatic compression feature adapts to changes in data distribution and access patterns over time, dynamically adjusting compression settings to maximize storage efficiency and query performance.

Overall, data compression strategies in Snowflake offer a powerful mechanism for optimizing storage utilization and query performance within the platform. By leveraging columnar compression, block-level compression, and automatic compression features, organizations can minimize storage costs, improve data transfer speeds, and enhance overall system efficiency, enabling faster and more scalable data processing workflows within Snowflake.

CHAPTER 9

Working with Laravel 10

Laravel is a robust and elegant PHP framework that simplifies web application development by providing a rich set of features, tools, and conventions. It offers a clean and expressive syntax, along with a wide range of built-in functionalities, making it a popular choice for building modern web applications. In this chapter, we'll explore the fundamentals of Laravel 10 and how to set up a development environment to get started with Laravel development.

To begin working with Laravel, the first step is to set up a development environment on your local machine. Laravel provides a convenient tool called Composer, a dependency manager for PHP, to install and manage Laravel projects. Start by installing Composer if you haven't already done so, then use it to create a new Laravel project using the Laravel installer or Composer's create-project command. This will generate a new Laravel project with the necessary directory structure and files to get you started.

Once you have created a new Laravel project, you can use Laravel's artisan command-line interface to manage your application, run built-in development servers, and generate boilerplate code. Laravel's extensive documentation provides detailed instructions on how to use artisan commands for various tasks, such as creating controllers, models, migrations, and routes. Additionally, Laravel's configuration files,

© Ronald Steelman 2024
R. Steelman, *Mastering the Snowflake SQL API with Laravel 10*, Apress Pocket Guides,
https://doi.org/10.1007/979-8-8688-0382-6_9

located in the config directory, allow you to customize various aspects of your application, such as database connections, caching, and session management.

Furthermore, Laravel provides a powerful ORM (object relational mapping) called Eloquent, which simplifies database interactions by providing a fluent query builder and ActiveRecord implementation. With Eloquent, you can define database models that represent your application's data entities and use them to perform database operations, such as querying, inserting, updating, and deleting records. Laravel's migration system allows you to define and manage database schema changes using PHP code, making it easy to version control and deploy database changes across different environments.

In summary, Laravel is a versatile and powerful PHP framework that streamlines web application development with its expressive syntax, rich feature set, and extensive documentation. By following the steps outlined in this chapter to set up a Laravel development environment and familiarizing yourself with Laravel's key concepts and tools, you'll be well-equipped to start building modern web applications with Laravel 10.

Exploring Laravel 10 Fundamentals

Exploring Laravel 10 fundamentals is essential for understanding the core concepts and features of the framework, laying a solid foundation for building robust web applications. At its core, Laravel embraces the model-view-controller (MVC) architectural pattern, which separates application logic into distinct layers for improved maintainability and scalability. In Laravel, controllers handle incoming HTTP requests, models interact with the application's data layer, and views render the user interface.

One fundamental aspect of Laravel is its routing system, which maps HTTP request URIs to controller actions. Laravel provides a concise and expressive syntax for defining routes using the routes/web.php file. For example, you can define a route to handle GET requests to the /users URI by associating it with a UserController method.

Listing 9-1. Laravel REST API—GET

```
Route::get('/users', 'App\Http\Controllers\UserController@
index');
```

Furthermore, Laravel's Eloquent ORM simplifies database interactions by providing a fluent query builder and ActiveRecord implementation. With Eloquent, you can define database models that represent your application's data entities and use them to perform database operations. For instance, consider a user model that represents users in your application.

Listing 9-2. Laravel user model

```
use Illuminate\Database\Eloquent\Model;

class User extends Model
{
    //
}
```

You can then use this model to perform database operations, such as querying for users:

```
$users = User::where('status', 'active')->get();
```

Moreover, Laravel's Blade templating engine offers a powerful and intuitive way to create dynamic views. Blade templates allow you to write clean and readable PHP code within your views, making it easy to work with data and control structures. For example, you can use Blade directives such as @foreach to iterate over arrays and collections.

Listing 9-3. Laravel user loop

```
@foreach ($users as $user)
    <p>{{ $user->name }}</p>
@endforeach
```

Additionally, Laravel provides a rich ecosystem of built-in features and utilities that streamline common web development tasks. For instance, Laravel's authentication system offers pre-built authentication scaffolding, including user registration, login, and password reset functionality. By running a single artisan command, you can generate all the necessary controllers, views, and routes for authentication:

```
php artisan make:auth
```

Overall, exploring Laravel 10 fundamentals introduces developers to the key concepts and tools that empower them to build modern and maintainable web applications. By mastering Laravel's routing system, Eloquent ORM, Blade templating engine, and built-in features, developers can leverage the full potential of the framework to create elegant and efficient web solutions.

Leveraging Laravel 10 Tools and Features

Leveraging Laravel 10's tools and features empowers developers to build sophisticated and efficient web applications with ease. In this section, we'll explore some of the most powerful tools and features offered by Laravel 10 and how they can be used to streamline development workflows and enhance productivity.

One of the standout features of Laravel 10 is its robust authentication system, which provides pre-built scaffolding for user registration, login, and password reset functionality. By simply running the artisan command php artisan make:auth, developers can generate all the necessary controllers, views, and routes for user authentication. This saves developers significant time and effort, allowing them to focus on building the core features of their application without having to reinvent the wheel.

Another powerful tool in Laravel 10 is its built-in task scheduling capabilities, powered by the artisan command schedule:run. With Laravel's task scheduler, developers can define scheduled tasks using expressive syntax similar to cron jobs. For example, developers can schedule recurring tasks such as sending email reminders, generating reports, or clearing cached data. Laravel's task scheduler ensures that these tasks are executed automatically at predefined intervals, helping to automate routine maintenance tasks and improve application reliability.

Furthermore, Laravel's robust testing support, facilitated by PHPUnit, enables developers to write comprehensive unit and feature tests for their applications. Laravel provides a suite of testing utilities and assertions that make it easy to write and execute tests, ensuring that code changes do not introduce regressions or break existing functionality. For example, developers can use Laravel's HTTP testing tools to simulate HTTP requests and verify that routes and controllers behave as expected.

Additionally, Laravel's artisan command-line interface offers a wide range of utilities for managing application assets, running database migrations, generating code scaffolds, and more. For example, developers can use the artisan command php artisan make:model to generate Eloquent models or php artisan migrate to run database migrations and synchronize the database schema with changes in the application's codebase. Laravel's artisan commands streamline common development tasks, making it easy for developers to perform routine operations and maintain code consistency throughout the development lifecycle.

Overall, leveraging Laravel 10's tools and features empowers developers to build high-quality web applications efficiently and effectively. By harnessing Laravel's authentication system, task scheduler, testing support, and artisan command-line interface, developers can accelerate development workflows, automate routine tasks, and deliver robust and reliable web solutions that meet the needs of modern businesses and users.

CHAPTER 10

Architectural Patterns and Solutions

This chapter delves into the various architectural patterns and best practices for designing scalable and efficient data solutions using Snowflake. Snowflake's unique architecture, which separates compute and storage layers, offers unparalleled flexibility and scalability, making it ideal for handling diverse data workloads and use cases. In this chapter, we'll explore some common architectural patterns and solutions that leverage Snowflake's capabilities to address different data processing challenges.

One architectural pattern commonly used with Snowflake is the data lakehouse architecture, which combines the strengths of data lakes and data warehouses to provide a unified platform for storing and analyzing structured and semi-structured data. With Snowflake's native support for semi-structured data formats such as JSON, Avro, and Parquet, organizations can ingest and analyze diverse data types within the same data warehouse environment. This allows for greater flexibility and agility in data processing, as organizations can store raw data in its native format and perform on-the-fly transformations and analyses using SQL and other analytics tools.

Another architectural pattern is the data mart approach, where organizations create specialized data marts tailored to specific business units or use cases within the larger data warehouse environment. Snowflake's multi-cluster architecture and virtual data sharing capabilities

R. Steelman, *Mastering the Snowflake SQL API with Laravel 10*, Apress Pocket Guides, https://doi.org/10.1007/979-8-8688-0382-6_10

enable organizations to create isolated data marts with dedicated compute resources, ensuring optimal performance and resource utilization. By partitioning data into separate data marts, organizations can streamline data access and analysis for different user groups while maintaining centralized governance and control over data assets.

Additionally, Snowflake's support for real-time data processing and streaming analytics enables organizations to build event-driven architectures that ingest, process, and analyze streaming data in real time. With integrations with streaming platforms such as Apache Kafka and AWS Kinesis, Snowflake allows organizations to ingest and process high-velocity data streams at scale, enabling real-time decision-making and actionable insights. This architectural pattern is particularly useful for use cases such as IoT (Internet of Things) analytics, fraud detection, and real-time monitoring.

Furthermore, Snowflake's extensibility and integration capabilities enable organizations to integrate with third-party tools and services to enhance their data solutions further. For example, organizations can leverage Snowflake's native integrations with BI (business intelligence) tools such as Tableau, Looker, and Power BI to visualize and analyze data directly within the Snowflake environment. Additionally, Snowflake's support for data sharing and cross-cloud data exchange enables organizations to collaborate with external partners and share data securely across organizational boundaries, facilitating data-driven decision-making and insights.

By understanding and leveraging Snowflake's unique architecture, organizations can build data solutions that meet their evolving business needs, drive innovation, and unlock the full potential of their data assets. Let's take a look at a few of these patterns.

In data lakehouse architecture, this pattern allows organizations to leverage Snowflake's capabilities to unify data lakes and data warehouses. Raw data from various sources, including structured and semi-structured formats, is ingested into Snowflake's data lake storage layer. Snowflake's ability to natively handle semi-structured data allows for flexible storage and analysis without the need for preprocessing. Users can then query and analyze this data using Snowflake's SQL interface, combining the scalability of a data lake with the query performance of a data warehouse.

In a data mart approach, organizations can adopt a data mart approach to create specialized data repositories tailored to specific business units or use cases. Using Snowflake's multi-cluster architecture, organizations can provision dedicated compute resources for each data mart, ensuring optimal performance and resource utilization. For example, a sales data mart may contain data specifically curated for sales analytics, while a finance data mart may focus on financial reporting and analysis. This approach allows for granular control over data access and analysis while maintaining centralized governance.

An approach unique to Snowflake, we can look at data sharing and collaboration approaches. Snowflake's data sharing and cross-cloud data exchange capabilities facilitate collaboration and data sharing across organizational boundaries. For example, a retail chain can securely share sales data with its suppliers, enabling better demand forecasting and inventory management. Additionally, organizations can leverage Snowflake's native integrations with BI tools like Tableau or Looker to visualize and analyze data directly within the Snowflake environment, streamlining the analytics workflow and enabling faster decision-making.

CHAPTER 11

Community and Resources

This chapter serves as a gateway to the wealth of support, knowledge, and collaboration opportunities available within the Snowflake ecosystem. Snowflake's vibrant community comprises a diverse network of users, developers, data professionals, and experts who actively engage in discussions, share insights, and contribute to the collective understanding of Snowflake's best practices and use cases. This chapter introduces readers to the various resources, forums, and community-driven initiatives that they can leverage to enhance their Snowflake journey.

From official documentation and tutorials to community forums and user groups, Snowflake offers a plethora of resources to help users navigate the platform effectively. Readers will discover how to access comprehensive documentation, step-by-step tutorials, and self-paced training modules provided by Snowflake, enabling them to gain proficiency in using Snowflake's features and functionalities. Moreover, the chapter highlights the importance of community-driven initiatives such as Snowflake Community Office Hours, virtual meetups, and online forums where users can seek help, share insights, and collaborate with peers to address challenges and explore innovative solutions using Snowflake.

© Ronald Steelman 2024
R. Steelman, *Mastering the Snowflake SQL API with Laravel 10*, Apress Pocket Guides,
https://doi.org/10.1007/979-8-8688-0382-6_11

Snowflake Community and User Groups

The Snowflake community is a vibrant and inclusive ecosystem comprised of users, developers, data professionals, and experts who actively contribute to the collective knowledge and growth of the platform. At the heart of this community are the Snowflake data heroes, a group of dedicated individuals recognized for their expertise, contributions, and advocacy within the Snowflake ecosystem. These data heroes play a pivotal role in fostering collaboration, sharing best practices, and providing guidance to fellow users through various channels such as community forums, webinars, and events.

Through their active engagement and advocacy, Snowflake data heroes help empower users to maximize the value of Snowflake's cloud data platform, driving innovation and excellence in data management and analytics. They actively participate in community-driven initiatives, share their expertise and insights, and provide support and guidance to users at all levels of expertise. By championing collaboration and knowledge-sharing, Snowflake data heroes contribute to the growth and success of the Snowflake community, inspiring others to unlock the full potential of data with Snowflake.

Snowflake user groups are vibrant communities of like-minded professionals, enthusiasts, and experts who gather to exchange ideas, share best practices, and network with peers who share an interest in leveraging Snowflake's cloud data platform. These user groups span across various regions and industries, offering members valuable opportunities to connect with fellow users, learn from each other's experiences, and stay updated on the latest trends and developments in the world of Snowflake.

Whether through in-person meetups, virtual events, or online forums, Snowflake user groups provide a platform for members to collaborate, problem-solve, and gain insights into how others are using Snowflake to drive innovation and solve real-world challenges. These groups often host guest speakers, organize workshops, and facilitate discussions on topics ranging from technical deep dives and best practices to industry-specific use cases and case studies. By fostering a sense of community and collaboration, Snowflake user groups empower members to expand their skills, grow their networks, and make meaningful contributions to the broader Snowflake ecosystem.

Learning Resources and Training

Snowflake offers a comprehensive array of learning resources and training programs designed to empower users to master the platform and unleash the full potential of their data. At the core of Snowflake's learning ecosystem is the Snowflake learning portal, a centralized hub where users can access a wide range of self-paced courses, tutorials, and documentation covering various aspects of Snowflake's features and functionalities. From beginner-level tutorials to advanced certification programs, the learning portal caters to users at all skill levels and backgrounds, providing them with the knowledge and skills needed to excel in data management and analytics.

In addition to the learning portal, Snowflake also offers instructor-led training programs and workshops conducted by experienced instructors and industry experts. These training sessions provide participants with hands-on experience and practical insights into using Snowflake's platform effectively. Whether through virtual classrooms or on-site training sessions, Snowflake's instructor-led training programs offer a personalized and interactive learning experience, allowing participants to engage with instructors, ask questions, and collaborate with peers in real-time.

Furthermore, Snowflake's community-driven approach to learning extends beyond formal training programs, with a wealth of resources and support available through community forums, user groups, and knowledge-sharing initiatives. Users can leverage community forums such as Snowflake Community Office Hours and online user groups to seek help, share insights, and collaborate with peers on common challenges and use cases. Additionally, Snowflake hosts regular webinars, virtual meetups, and events featuring guest speakers and industry leaders, providing users with valuable opportunities to stay updated on the latest trends and best practices in data management and analytics. Through these diverse learning resources and training programs, Snowflake empowers users to unlock the full potential of their data and drive innovation in their organizations.

Snowflake Certification

Snowflake certifications are prestigious credentials that validate an individual's proficiency and expertise in using the Snowflake platform for data management and analytics. With a range of certification exams available, Snowflake offers professionals the opportunity to demonstrate their mastery of various aspects of the platform, from core concepts and fundamentals to advanced analytics and administration skills. Achieving Snowflake certification not only enhances an individual's credibility and marketability but also signifies their commitment to excellence in data management and analytics.

Snowflake certifications cover a broad spectrum of topics and skill levels, catering to users at different stages of their Snowflake journey. For beginners, the SnowPro Core Certification serves as an entry-level credential that validates foundational knowledge of Snowflake's features, architecture, and best practices. As users progress in their Snowflake proficiency, they can pursue more advanced certifications such as the SnowPro Advanced Certification, which focuses on specialized areas such as data modeling, performance optimization, and security administration.

Moreover, Snowflake certifications are recognized and respected by organizations worldwide, serving as a benchmark for hiring, promotion, and career advancement in the field of data management and analytics. Employers value Snowflake-certified professionals for their demonstrated expertise and ability to leverage Snowflake's platform to drive business value and innovation. Additionally, Snowflake's certification program offers a structured learning path and study resources to help candidates prepare for exams, including official study guides, practice exams, and training courses. By earning Snowflake certifications, professionals can distinguish themselves in a competitive job market and unlock new opportunities for career growth and advancement in the dynamic field of data management and analytics.

CHAPTER 12

Conclusion

Our journey through the Snowflake SQL API has been a comprehensive exploration of Snowflake's powerful capabilities and features for data management and analytics. Throughout this book, readers have gained insights into Snowflake's unique architecture, SQL functionality, and best practices for designing scalable and efficient data solutions. From understanding the fundamentals of SQL querying to mastering advanced techniques for performance tuning and optimization, readers have acquired the knowledge and skills needed to harness the full potential of Snowflake's cloud data platform.

As organizations increasingly rely on data-driven insights to inform decision-making and drive innovation, the importance of mastering Snowflake's platform cannot be overstated. With its scalable, secure, and flexible architecture, Snowflake empowers organizations to unlock the value of their data and derive actionable insights that fuel growth and competitive advantage. By leveraging Snowflake's capabilities for data warehousing, data lake integration, and real-time analytics, organizations can gain a holistic view of their data landscape and make informed decisions that drive business success.

Moreover, the Snowflake community and ecosystem play a crucial role in supporting and empowering users on their Snowflake journey. From community forums and user groups to certifications and training programs, Snowflake offers a wealth of resources and support to help users maximize their productivity and success with the platform. By engaging

© Ronald Steelman 2024
R. Steelman, *Mastering the Snowflake SQL API with Laravel 10*, Apress Pocket Guides,
https://doi.org/10.1007/979-8-8688-0382-6_12

with the Snowflake community, sharing insights, and collaborating with peers, users can stay updated on the latest trends and best practices in data management and analytics, driving continuous learning and improvement.

This book covering the Snowflake SQL API serves as a comprehensive guide and reference for professionals seeking to unlock the full potential of Snowflake's cloud data platform. Whether you are a beginner looking to get started with Snowflake or an experienced user seeking to deepen your understanding of advanced SQL techniques and best practices, this book provides the knowledge, tools, and resources needed to excel in the dynamic field of data management and analytics with Snowflake. As organizations continue to embrace data-driven strategies and digital transformation initiatives, mastering Snowflake's platform will be essential for driving innovation, unlocking new opportunities, and achieving sustainable growth in the digital age.

We will look at two final topics in this book to help readers in their journey with Snowflake and where they should be looking for the future of data warehousing, Snowflake, and application integration.

The Transformative Power of Snowflake SQL API

The transformative power of Snowflake's SQL API lies in its ability to democratize data access and enable organizations to unlock the full potential of their data assets. By providing a unified platform for data warehousing, data lake integration, and real-time analytics, Snowflake empowers organizations to break down data silos, streamline data workflows, and derive actionable insights that drive business success. With Snowflake's SQL API, users can leverage familiar SQL syntax to query and analyze data across diverse data sources, enabling faster decision-making and greater agility in responding to changing business needs.

Furthermore, Snowflake's cloud-native architecture and scalable infrastructure offer unparalleled flexibility and scalability, allowing organizations to scale their data operations seamlessly as their data volumes and analytics workloads grow. Whether processing terabytes or petabytes of data, Snowflake's elastic compute resources and on-demand pricing model ensure that organizations can scale up or down according to their needs, without the need for complex infrastructure management or capacity planning. This scalability empowers organizations to innovate faster, iterate more efficiently, and stay ahead of the competition in today's fast-paced digital landscape.

Moreover, Snowflake's commitment to security, reliability, and performance ensures that organizations can trust their most critical data workloads to the platform with confidence. With built-in features such as encryption, role-based access control, and data governance capabilities, Snowflake provides organizations with the tools and controls needed to protect sensitive data and comply with regulatory requirements. Additionally, Snowflake's continuous innovation and investment in performance optimization ensure that users can achieve fast query response times and high throughput, even with complex analytics workloads.

The transformative power of Snowflake's SQL API lies in its ability to empower organizations to harness the full potential of their data for strategic advantage. By providing a unified, scalable, and secure platform for data management and analytics, Snowflake enables organizations to accelerate innovation, drive growth, and achieve digital transformation at scale. As organizations continue to embrace data-driven strategies and leverage the latest technologies to gain insights and competitive advantage, Snowflake's SQL API will remain a foundational tool for unlocking the value of data and driving business success in the modern era.

Looking Ahead: The Future of Snowflake

Looking ahead, the future of Snowflake appears promising as the platform continues to innovate and evolve to meet the ever-changing needs of organizations in the digital age. With a relentless focus on driving customer success and enabling data-driven decision-making, Snowflake is poised to play a central role in shaping the future of data management and analytics. As organizations increasingly rely on data to drive innovation, improve efficiency, and gain competitive advantage, Snowflake's cloud-native architecture and scalable infrastructure will continue to provide a solid foundation for organizations to build and scale their data operations.

One of the key areas where Snowflake is expected to make significant advancements is in the realm of artificial intelligence (AI) and machine learning (ML). By integrating AI and ML capabilities directly into the Snowflake platform, organizations will be able to leverage advanced analytics and predictive modeling to gain deeper insights into their data and uncover new opportunities for growth and innovation. This integration will enable organizations to democratize AI and ML capabilities, making them accessible to users across the organization and driving innovation at scale.

Additionally, Snowflake is poised to continue expanding its ecosystem of partnerships and integrations with leading technology providers, enabling organizations to leverage best-of-breed solutions for their data management and analytics needs. By collaborating with industry leaders in areas such as data governance, data integration, and business intelligence, Snowflake will further enhance its platform's capabilities and provide users with a seamless and integrated experience for managing and analyzing their data.

Furthermore, Snowflake is committed to driving sustainability and corporate responsibility initiatives that align with its mission to empower organizations to make informed decisions and drive positive change. As organizations increasingly prioritize sustainability and social

126

responsibility, Snowflake's commitment to environmental stewardship and ethical data practices will become increasingly important. By investing in renewable energy, reducing carbon emissions, and promoting ethical data usage, Snowflake will continue to lead by example and inspire others to follow suit in creating a more sustainable and responsible future for data management and analytics.

Index

A

Accessing Snowflake SQL API
   AWS Secrets Manager, 39
   GitHub key, 39
   JWT expiration, 40
   Laravel 10, 32
   public and private key, 39
   Snowflake service, 32–39
   SSH key, 39
   standard SQL queries, 32
Account identifiers, 16, 17
Advanced SQL techniques
   data transformation, 69–73
   dynamic SQL, 75–77
   handling date and time
      data, 73–75
   stored procedures, 76–78
   UDFs, 78, 79
Aggregate functions, 62, 63
AJAX, 14
Amazon Web Services (AWS), 11
Apache Kafka, 114
Architectural patterns, 113–115
Artificial intelligence (AI), 126
Audit trail, 82
Authentication, 82–84
Authorization, 82–84

Average function (AVG), 62
AWS Kinesis, 114
AWS Secrets Manager, 39

B

Bind variables, 66, 67
Black Diamond, 27
Blade templates, 109
Business intelligence (BI) tool, 114,
     115, 126

C

Caching query, 97
CASE statement, 69–71
class_grades, 57
Classic UI, 20
Cloud-based service, 11
Cloud storage services, 11
Clustering keys, 101, 102
COALESCE statement, 71–73
Community-driven approach, 119
Community-driven initiatives, 118
Composer, 107
Confidentiality, 81
config_version_deployed, 52
CROSS JOIN, 59, 60
CTEs, 64–66

© Ronald Steelman 2024
R. Steelman, *Mastering the Snowflake SQL API with Laravel 10*, Apress Pocket Guides,
https://doi.org/10.1007/979-8-8688-0382-6